FANCY BEER

*Beer-Topia*

GRAB A
COLD ONE

*Beer-Topia*

"You from within our glasses, you lusty golden brew, whoever imbibes takes fire from you. The young and the old sing your praises. Here's to beer, here's to cheer, here's to beer."

—**Bedrich Smetana**, *The Bartered Bride* (1865)

## UNCLE JOHN'S BEER-TOPIA

Portable Press is an imprint of the Printers Row Publishing Group
A Division of Readerlink Distribution Services, LLC

"Bathroom Reader," "Portable Press," and "Bathroom Readers' Institute" are registered trademarks of Readerlink Distribution Services, LLC.
All rights reserved

For information, write: The Bathroom Readers' Institute,
P.O. Box 1117, Ashland, OR 97520
www.bathroomreader.com

Cover and interior design by Andy Taray – Ohioboy.com

Library of Congress Cataloging-in-Publication Data

Uncle John's beer-topia.
    pages cm
  ISBN 978-1-62686-359-0 (hardcover)
1. Beer--Humor. 2. Beer--Anecdotes. I. Bathroom Readers' Institute (Ashland, Or.) II. Title: Beer-vana.
  PN6231.B43U53 2015
  818'.607--dc23
  2014041247

Printed in the United States of America
First Printing: March 2015
1 2 3 4 5   19 18 17 16 15

Beer-Topia

4

# THANK YOU!

The Bathroom Readers' Institute sincerely thanks the people whose advice and assistance made this book possible.

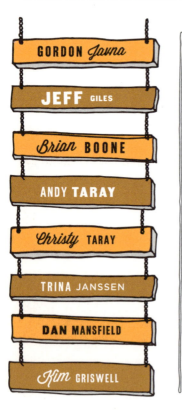

GORDON *Javna*

**JEFF** GILES

*Brian* **BOONE**

ANDY **TARAY**

*Christy* TARAY

TRINA JANSSEN

**DAN** MANSFIELD

*Kim* GRISWELL

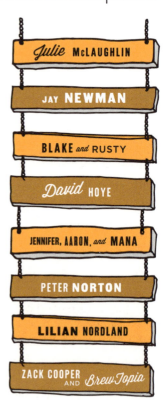

*Julie* McLAUGHLIN

JAY **NEWMAN**

**BLAKE** *and* RUSTY

*David* HOYE

JENNIFER, AARON, *and* **MANA**

PETER **NORTON**

**LILIAN** NORDLAND

ZACK COOPER *and* *BrewTopia*

*Beer-Topia*

# CONTENTS

Ale vs. Lager .................................................. 11

A Guide to Ales ............................................. 12

The Beer Taster's Glossary of Terms ..................... 17

What Makes a Beer a Beer? ........................... 19

A Child's Garden of Malt Trivia ........................... 21

Ancient Beer ................................................ 23

Beers That Went Flat ..................................... 27

The Proper Glass .......................................... 31

The Craft Beer Revolution .............................. 35

It's Oktoberfest! ............................................ 45

Beer by the Numbers ..................................... 46

A Child's Garden of Hops Trivia ......................... 48

How to Talk Like a Brewer .............................. 51

For Your Health! ............................................ 57

Strange Beer Flavors ...................................... 59

Totally Necessary Beer Gadgets .........................65

83 Funny Craft Beer Names ........................70

A Guide to Lagers .........................74

Something in the Water .........................77

The Beer Belly: Fact or Fiction? .........................79

Beer Under Prohibition .........................81

How to Open a Beer Without
 a Bottle Opener .........................84

A Toast to Andre the Giant .........................86

44 Hops Varieties with Cool Names .........................88

The World's Most Expensive Beers .........................90

Who Owns What .........................93

Hair of the Dog .........................97

Better Living Through Packaging .........................100

The Universal Language .........................104

Beer Treats .........................106

The United States of Beer, Part 1 .........................109

7

Billy Beer ...............................................114

The Wisdom of Billy Carter..................116

Make Your Own Beer in Two Hours..................117

More Strange Beer Flavors................................124

Very Old Drinking Games...............................125

Beers Named After Great
    Writers and Artists................................129

More of the World's Most Expensive Beers .........133

Your Dad's Beer, Part 1 .....................................137

Beer Is Good for You! ........................................145

Beer Movies..........................................147

The Hows and Whys of Nonalcoholic Beer..........151

The Most Popular Beers on Earth.....................156

A Beer for Everything........................................158

The United States of Beer, Part 2.....................161

Beers Named After Musicians ..........................166

Zombie Beer ...............................................169

Beer-Topia

Make It a Lite.................................................... 171

Beer Myths, Debunked.................................... 177

Hangovers: How Do They Work? ................... 179

Beer Math........................................................ 181

Destination: Beer ........................................... 183

Beers from TV ................................................ 191

"Hooray Beer!"............................................... 192

This Bud(s) for You ........................................ 194

A Beer Mixtape .............................................. 199

The United States of Beer, Part 3................... 201

Funny (and Real) British Pub Names .............. 206

Weights & Measures ...................................... 208

The Goats Who Loved Beer............................ 209

Your Dad's Beer, Part 2 ................................. 211

Running on Beer ............................................ 217

Pilgrim Pride................................................... 218

Everything's Fining ............................................. 220

The World's Top Beerhounds ............................. 221

Beer Meets Caffeine ........................................... 223

The United States of Beer, Part 4 ..................... 225

8 Odd Beer Laws ................................................. 230

Bear-Topia .......................................................... 231

The London Beer Flood ...................................... 234

Canadian Beer Cocktails .................................... 235

The Perfect Pour ................................................ 237

Can't Get Enough of that Wonderful Duff ...... 238

The Dry Beer Fad ............................................... 240

Breweriana ......................................................... 241

The United States of Beer, Part 5 ..................... 243

Washington's Tab ............................................... 249

Thinking of Beer ................................................ 250

Answers ............................................................... 254

Beer-Topia

# CHEERS!

**We're in the middle of a beer revolution.** There's nothing wrong with that canned stuff people used to drink at the bowling alley, but beer is a whole new animal these days. We're talking about the rich, intricate concoction brewed in small batches by innovative brewers all across the nation. And these brewers are true heroes, carefully selecting everything that goes into our beer, from the water, to the hops, to the goofy name they slap on the label. The world of beer has become, in short, a *Beer-Topia*. (Just like the name of this book!) And as it turns out, it's almost as much fun to read about beer as it is to drink it. (Almost.) So pour yourself a glass of beer-flavored words. Some of what's on tap:

- The best local beer in every state
- How to perfectly pour a beer, and into just the right glass
- The strangest-tasting and most expensive beers
- What's really in a beer, and who really made it
- And barrels more!

Whether you're a seasoned beer snob, a novice, or a homebrewer, there's something for you in the *Beer-Topia*.

—UNCLE JOHN AND THE BATHROOM READERS' INSTITUTE

# ALE VS. LAGER

Despite all the hundreds if not thousands of varieties of beer out there, there are really only two main types of beer: ales and lagers. On the great beer family tree, this is the basic fork that divides every drink, and it all comes down to the brewing process.

**Ales** are made with "top-fermenting" yeast, which is active at higher temperatures—around 60 to 75 degrees Fahrenheit—and ferment quicker, usually over a week or so, but sometimes even less. They also produce *esters*, the fruity or flowery scents detected by drinkers with refined palates.

**Lagers,** meanwhile, are brewed using "bottom-fermenting" yeast, which is active in colder climes (around 34 degrees). These drinks mature more slowly, in cold storage, and tend to have a hoppier flavor profile.

# A GUIDE TO ALES

**Wheat Beer/Hefeweizen.** The granddaddy of beer, this brew is generally regarded as the oldest style that still has any sort of widespread popularity, and it's pretty much what it sounds like: beer brewed with a mixture of wheat and barley. The traditional recipe, still used to produce Bavarian hefeweizen, calls for a 50/50 blend between the two, although wheat can gobble up a much higher percentage, plus noble hops, ale yeast, and water. Low on hops flavor and generally "softer" than some of its cousins in the ale family, it tends to possess a cloudy appearance due to the wheat proteins in the brew, both in its traditional form and in Belgium, where unmalted wheat is combined with spices to produce "white beers" such as Hoegaarden.

**Pale Ale.** This is a broad term used to describe all kinds of beer, but it all got its start in the early 18th century. Some frustrated brewers at

the Burton-on-Trent brewery in England started looking for alternatives to wood-fired kilns, whose unpredictable heat gave barley too dark a roast and often scorched the inventory. Turning to coke (processed coal) for their new heat supply, they discovered it was easier to control, allowing for a lighter roast—and in turn, a paler beer. In the UK, if you hear someone refer to a "pint of bitter," that's pale ale, and it ranges from low-alcohol by volume light brews (occasionally referred to as "boys' bitter") to the higher alcohol ends of the spectrum, spanning "ordinary" to "premium" and "best" bitters. Elsewhere in the world, pale ales tend to diverge from the maltier British brews; in the U.S., they can be almost as hoppy as India pale ales while still maintaining that light brown hue.

**India Pale Ale.** The IPA has its roots in England's colonial occupation

of India—a time when beer storage techniques weren't quite as refined as they are today. British citizens living in India found it difficult to get their hands on ale from the homeland because it tended to spoil during the long, oversea voyage from point A to point B. The solution? Load the stuff up with hops, whose preservative characteristics kept the beer from spoiling while adding a very distinctive flavor. Long thought of as strictly a regional drink, IPA found its way back to Great Britain in 1827. A ship bound for India wrecked off the coast of England, forcing the brewing company to sell its stock locally and starting the long process that ended with that bottle of Sierra Nevada (or one of the dozens of other popular microbrew IPAs) in your hand.

**Porter.** A dark brew with a robust chocolate or coffee flavor but little of the bitterness of stout, porter was once one of the world's most popular types of beer, but fell out of favor after pale ales and pilsners started taking over. During Prohibition in the U.S., it essentially disappeared,

but made a healthy comeback during the micro-brew explosion.

**Stout.** The exact origins of this style are difficult to pin down, but many believe it developed as an offshoot of porter; stronger brews were referred to as "stout porters." Thick and creamy, with a foamy head, this is the type of beer you're drinking when you enjoy a Guinness. And unless you're drinking from one of those Guinness cans or bottles with the gas cartridges inside, you'll probably have a more satisfying experience if you have this stuff on draught, because the nitrogen/carbon dioxide combo ("beer gas") that taps use produces the thick head and silky-smooth finish that makes a stout a stout.

**Brown Ale.** As with pale ales, this is a fairly broad term that encompasses beers across the ABV spectrum; you can find a brown ale that's gentle and sweet just as easily as you can find one that's hoppy and highly carbonated. Overall, however, they all tend to boast a fairly malty flavor, with

Beer-Topia

hops relegated to the margins—a characteristic that makes them easy to pair with a wide variety of foods. The next time the boss comes over for dinner and you're looking for something to serve with the meal, a brown ale (such as Newcastle) is a safe choice.

**Barleywine.** As you might suspect given its name, this variety tends to be aged longer than your average beer…and it's a heck of a lot more robust, too. Produced using recipes that call for long boils and tons of grain, barleywines are some of the more flavorful (and alcoholic) beers you can buy. However, as with other styles, the overall taste can vary substantially between American and European brews; in the UK, barleywines tend to have a maltier flavor, while in the U.S., they can be quite a bit hoppier. Either way, this is beer for those in search of a strong—and potentially very bitter—beer.

# THE BEER TASTER'S GLOSSARY OF TERMS

**Quaff.** A deep sip from a glass of beer.

**Lace.** The bits of foam left on the sides of a glass immediately after a quaff.

**Session beer.** A beer that's low in alcohol, generally around 4 percent. If you can have more than one in a sitting, or "session," and not get too tipsy, then you've been drinking a session beer.

**Musty.** A polite way to say that a beer tastes terrible because it has oxidized.

**Head retention.** A beer snob's way of measuring how fast an inch of foam collapses on top of a glass of beer.

**Hang.** If you're sitting around during a tasting session and you hear a drinker refer to "hang," that's

the sign of a persistently bitter beer with a harsh, lingering aftertaste.

**Mouthfeel.** A way to describe a beer's physical consistency on the tongue. As with most things of this nature, it's subjective and a reflection of individual palate.

**Astringency.** A mouth-puckering flavor that's a beer snob's fancy way of saying, "Gross, yuck, spit it out." It is likely stale, or "skunked."

**Chill haze.** The cloudy appearance that results when the proteins and tannins in beer glom onto each other during the cooling process. The way unfiltered wheat beer like Hoegaarden looks? That's chill haze.

**Chlorophenolic.** If you happen to be drinking with a big-time beer snob and you find that your brew smells like plastic, you can score points by describing it as "chlorophenolic." (Then send it back.)

# WHAT MAKES A BEER A BEER?

It's one of those things we never really have to think about, given that beer comes to us ready to drink in bottles, mugs, and cans. **But what is it, exactly, that sets beer apart from wine, for example, or whiskey?**

Simply defined, it comes down to three things: malted grain, yeast, and water. It's a lot more complicated than that, of course—turning those three things (and whatever else gets thrown into the mix for flavor) is the science of brewing. But whatever your favorite variety, it starts with those three ingredients.

Of course, beer hardly has a monopoly on those ingredients; one or all of them pop up in any number of recipes throughout the liquor

kingdom. Wine, for instance, calls for yeast and water, but uses fruit instead of grain. And while traditionally made with potatoes, today's vodka is usually made using grain, but it's distilled instead of fermented.

On the other hand, once you've learned the ground rules, it can be fun to engage in a little lively debate when things get a bit more confusing. For instance, there's sake, the Japanese rice wine; since rice is a grain, many have wondered whether sake is technically a beer, even though it isn't carbonated and has a very different flavor. Or how about the ongoing argument between the traditionalists who insist "real" vodka must be made with grain, and the emerging wave of distillers who point out you can achieve similar results with anything from grapes to maple syrup?

BIG TASTE

**TALLBOY**

— *Topia* —

GRAB A **BIGGIN'**
750 ml

# A CHILD'S GARDEN OF MALT TRIVIA

• Developed using a process that's ultimately rather simple but still so convoluted that the first person to do it might as well have been some sort of warlock, malt is the result of taking grain (usually barley), soaking it until the seeds start to germinate, and then drying it. Why in the world would anyone do that to perfectly good baby plants, you ask? Simple: When you dry out the germinated grain (referred to as green malt), you're locking in sugar-producing enzymes that kick in during the brewing process, giving your yeast enough food to make alcohol.

• Green malt is dried before brewing, but this can be accomplished at different temperatures, and, depending on the heat and duration of the roast, you end up with malts that add remarkably different colors and flavors to beer. A lightly roasted malt with an ale yeast will produce a pale

or golden ale; coupled with a lager yeast, it'll produce a pilsner. Go a little darker, and you'll end up with an amber ale or a Märzen—darker still, and you get into brown ales, dark lagers, porters, stouts, and *schwarzbiers*, or black lagers.

• Not that we're suggesting beer is anyone's idea of a health food, but it does make use of some vitamin-rich ingredients, and barley might be at the top of that list: molybdenum, manganese, selenium, copper, vitamin B1, chromium, phosphorus, magnesium, and niacin are all found in the wonder grain, as well as fiber to help you poop.

• Malt isn't just used for beer. The unique way it gets friendly with yeast during the brewing process also makes it a great catalyst for other favorite drinks, including that precious single-malt scotch or whiskey your father-in-law doesn't like to share.

# ANCIENT BEER

When we say "ancient beer," we don't mean that one weird beer at the back of your fridge that someone brought over for a party but never got drank. Really, beer has been around for thousands of years, and while the exact circumstances of its birth have been lost in the sands of time, archaeologists and anthropologists have turned up some fascinating evidence in their quest to trace the origins and development of man's greatest invention.

Humans have been drinking fermented beverages for a very long time. And although this shouldn't surprise anyone, they didn't always taste much like the beer we know today. One, it was served at room temperature; two, it didn't include hops; and three, it was a heck of a lot thicker than your average ale. What the first brewers did use is up for debate, but the current evidence suggests that as far back as 9,000 years ago, the ancient Chinese mixed fermented rice with honey,

hawthorn, and other natural sweeteners. In Mesopotamia, beer started as bread loaves that were chopped up and soaked in water, stomped, strained, and flavored with an assortment of additives that included dates, honey, ginger, and mandrake root.

The Mesopotamians took their beer pretty seriously, believing their brewers—usually women—were protected by an array of deities that included Ninkasi, the goddess of alcohol. The first liquor laws showed up on the books in 2,100 BC, when the Babylonian king Hammurabi devoted a portion of his code to tavern regulations.

Of course, early brewing methods being what they were, the results could be highly variable. What passed for beer back then bears little resemblance to today's brews, not least because it was thick, not carbonated, and—in the case of

the ancient Sumerians—sipped through a straw. Plenty of drinkers felt the same way back then, too; in and around Rome, where grapes were abundant, beer never even remotely approached wine in popularity.

Elsewhere in Europe, however, beer reigned supreme—after the 13th century, when Bohemian brewers managed to fine-tune the addition of hops, which preserved the beer, in turn allowing for production and export on a far greater scale.

Not everyone appreciated it. In England, for a time, there was something of a standoff between traditional unhopped "ale" and the newfangled hoppy "beer," but by the 16th century, hops reigned supreme. This ascension was perhaps most notably reflected in the Reinheitsgebot, a "purity law" decreed in 1516 by William IV, Duke of Bavaria. This law mandated that beer be made only from water, barley, and hops (the addition of yeast was still about two centuries away).

All those eons of brewing helped lead to your favorite modern-day beers, but there are definitely drinkers who feel we may have lost a few things along the way—chief among them the experience of imbibing beverages blessed with the broader and more complex flavors that come from stuffing one's brew with the grab bags of herbs and spices used thousands of years ago. To that end, some brewers have started pursuing modern re-creations of ancient recipes painstakingly pieced together using information gleaned from archaeological digs. Dogfish Head's Ancient Ales line, assisted by anthropologist Patrick McGovern, includes beers such as Midas Touch ("based on molecular evidence found in a Turkish tomb believed to have belonged to King Midas") and Chateau Jiahu (brewed with ingredients "unearthed from a 9,000-year-old tomb in China").

Whether the old stuff tastes better or worse than your average 21st-century six-pack is totally up to your palate, of course.

# BEERS THAT WENT FLAT

**Nude Beer.** The most brilliant ideas are often the simplest, and the Golden Beverage Company's late, lamented Nude Beer is a perfect example of that principle in action. This '80s-era brew came bottled with a label picturing a lovely swimsuited lass whose minimal attire was made out of the same flaky metal stuff that covers scratch-off lottery tickets…and would therefore vanish completely when rubbed off with a coin or fingernail. It was interactive, it required physical exercise, and it encouraged the appreciation of beauty; unfortunately, it also ran afoul of many local decency laws, making it difficult to distribute or effectively market in many areas.

**Harley-Davidson Beer.** It's arguably a little unfair to include this brew here, given that it was only produced in limited quantities as part of the Daytona Week motorcycle festival, but whether or not it was intentional, Harley-Davidson Beer's failure to take the nation by storm seems like a missed opportunity, a macho response to the beer culture of the time, in which light (or "lite") beers were taking off and Bud Light was using pit bull Spuds MacKenzie as a mascot. This was especially true of the beer's 1987 and 1988 editions, which came in cans emblazoned "HEAVY BEER."

**Hop'n Gator Beer.** Taste is entirely subjective, and one man's swill is almost always bound to be another man's refreshing pleasure. That said, Hop'n Gator Beer sounds so disgusting that it's hard to believe it was ever actually a thing. The brainchild of Gatorade inventor Dr. Robert Cade, this justifiably short-lived beverage blended Cade's popular lemon-lime sports drink…with beer. Essentially a Gatorade shandy, it was only

Beer-Topia

bottled for a few years, from 1969 through 1972. Years later, the Iron City Brewing Company tried bottling their own version (a citrus malt liquor) before being sued into submission by Gatorade.

**Miller Clear.** The clear drink fad of the early '90s is chiefly remembered for spawning the persistent beverage punchlines—and marketplace flops—Zima and Crystal Pepsi. But if test market drinkers had just been a little more enthusiastic, we might have been treated to something even sillier: Miller Clear, a 4.6% ABV brew that *The Independent* described as looking like 7-Up and tasting "like a sweetened seltzer with the faintest touch of oily, medicinal hoppiness." Miller execs steadfastly denied that they were trying to hop on the transparent-beverage trend, insisting it was simply the accidental result of some distillery tinkering that produced what the ad campaign somewhat perplexingly promised was "good beer-drinking beer." Clearly, sales told a different story—like Crystal Pepsi, clear beer didn't make it past 1994.

**Miller Chill.** This Mexican-style beer offered a "hint of lime" and "pinch of salt" to produce "great light beer from America and the chelada-style from Mexico." Alas, despite being exhorted to "taste the thrill"—and, later, wooed with a rejiggered recipe that contained half as many carbs—consumers gave Miller Chill the cold shoulder in 2013.

**Tequiza.** One of the more high-concept experiments ever to tumble out of the Anheuser-Busch chute, Tequiza was billed as "beer with blue agave nectar and a natural flavor of imported tequila and lime." This description was just misleading enough to lure wacky-product enthusiasts into purchasing a random six-pack in the mistaken belief that they'd be drinking tequila-laced beer. It was really just slightly citrusy pale lager, like a Corona, but with lime already in it. But that was enough to keep it lingering in stores from 1998 to 2009, at which point it was phased out in favor of the considerably more male-friendly Bud Light Lime.

# THE PROPER GLASS

*Which glass goes with which beer?*

No matter what you're drinking out of, though, don't chill or freeze your glass! It might look like a classy move, but it has the nasty added effect of creating condensation, which dilutes your precious drink. (There is nothing wrong, however, with displaying your glassware in a special case under gallery lighting.)

**Pilsner glass.** Tall and tapered at the bottom, this long glass is good for highlighting the colors in one's brew while also preserving the head. Pairs well with pilsners, obviously, but it's also good for lagers, bocks, low-alcohol beers, and witbier.

Beer-Topia

**Goblet.** Not just an accessory for fairy-tale villains, the wine goblet is quite well suited for beer; in fact, many of them are made with bowls specially scored to help maintain a two-inch head on your drink. Next time you're pouring a strong and hearty Belgian brew, try a wide-mouthed chalice.

**Pint glass.** Every good pint deserves a pint glass, which is why this rivals the mug for the most versatile beer vessel money can buy. Whether you're holding the 16-ounce, the 20-ounce Imperial, or the German Becker style, it's hard to go wrong with a well-made pint glass.

**Weizen glass.** Similar to the pilsner glass, but wider at the top to make room for wheat beer's bigger head, this is what you want when you're pouring anything that makes you think about those amber waves of grain, whether it's hefeweizen or American wheat ale.

**Flute.** We tend to think of these guys as being solely for champagne, but their unique shape

helps preserve the carbonation of your brew while blasting all those volatiles into your face to make for a more intense, sensory drinking experience. Good for lambics as well as a variety of other beers, including American wild ales, bocks, pilsners, and dunkel lagers.

**Tulip.** Not just for tiptoeing through, the tulip is also a type of glass, and one whose delicate-looking shape actually acts as a sort of trap for your beer's volatiles—a fancy word for the hop oils and fermentation byproducts that add to the drink's unique scent while leaving room for the head to linger. Good for lambic, all kinds of Belgian or Scotch ales, saisons, and double or Imperial IPAs.

**Snifter.** Again, we tend to think of this glass as being made for something else—sipping cognac or brandy, in this case—but its unique shape also works well for strong ales,

with that wide bowl leaving extra room to swirl all those volatiles around while the tapered mouth helps keep them from wafting away too quickly. Good for barleywine, wheatwine, Belgian or American strong ales, and quads and tripels.

**Stange.** Kind of like a pilsner glass, it's thin (its name means "stick" in German), and its narrow body is supposed to help preserve the flavor characteristics of less pungent brews. Lambic, rye beer, bock, pilsner, and altbier all pair well with this glass.

**Wineglass.** The bowl shape is perfect for leaving headspace, and a wineglass's wide rim makes for a wonderfully aromatic experience if you're drinking something that has a unique nose. Reach for one of these standbys the next time you're pouring a Belgian ale, a black or Imperial stout, Imperial IPA, barleywine, or wheatwine because the punchier brews thrive in a bowl.

# THE CRAFT BEER REVOLUTION

You may not realize it, but right now might be the greatest time in history to be an American beer enthusiast. It's a time of unparalleled choices in a growing market with room for everything from polite, mass-market lagers to bigger, bolder, and weirder flavors brewed down the street or across town in small batches by passionate beer craftsfolk.

It wasn't all that long ago, let's say about 25 years, that "American beer" meant pretty much one thing, and it wasn't much to brag about; if you were a fancy beer drinker, you went for imported stuff. Today, the American beer industry is not only home to more small breweries than ever, it's producing brews that influence global beer trends, instead of the other way around.

So how did we get to this point? It's a fascinating story, and one that's far bigger than we have

space for here. But to get you started, here's an overview of how America went from a bustling beer garden to a macrobrew wasteland…and back again.

### MADE IN THE USA

As with many "distinctly American" phenomena, beer's domestic rise was immigrant-driven. German immigrants in the late 1800s, in particular, helped make it as popular as—if not more than—prevailing tipples such as rum, wine, and whiskey. Between the Civil War and World War I, breweries proliferated across the U.S., and with modern transportation, storage, and refrigeration technologies still in their infancies, beer was a relatively local beverage, with

brews generally available only in the areas where they were made. This could be frustrating for travelers who fell in love with a particular beer while passing through, but it also prevented market homogenization and made for a burgeoning and varied beer culture.

## A MINOR SETBACK

By the turn of the century, Americans were drinking about 20 gallons of beer per capita annually. That business was largely laid to waste by Prohibition, which culled a huge percentage of breweries right out of the market.

That thinning of the herd wasn't entirely Prohibition's fault—a growing thirst for lagers had already put a number of brewers out of business in the 50 years leading up to the passage of the law. Prohibition and the Great Depression proved devastating. At the end of 1933, around 750 breweries were in business; by 1950, that number had dropped to roughly 400. By 1960, only 200 remained.

## THE SILVER BULLET

Advances in refrigeration and packaging made it easier to ship beer longer distances, and the invention of the seven-ounce aluminum can by Bill Coors in 1959 represented another big step toward the kind of mass-market consistency promised by the major brewers. It also lured drinkers away from bars; by the end of the 1960s, more than 80 percent of all beer was sold in stores instead of on tap, and thanks to the advent of the supermarket and its attendant distribution system, it would only get easier for larger breweries to exert major influence over things like placement and cooler space.

## A SOLID ANCHOR

All of this spelled doom for small breweries, and by 1965, there was only one left in the U.S.: Anchor Brewing in San Francisco. Anchor was well on its way to bankruptcy, too, when it received an unexpected reprieve from Fritz Maytag III, great-grandson of the Maytag Corporation founder, who'd found himself looking for

something to do with his life (and his inheritance) after graduating from Stanford.

He found it in the struggling brewery, which he learned was near to closing when Frank Kuh, owner of the Old Spaghetti Factory (a major Anchor customer), told Maytag he should tour the grounds of the company before it shuttered. Although Kuh mentioned this mainly because he knew Maytag was a big fan of the beer, the visit ended with Maytag buying a 51 percent stake in the company and changing his life irrevocably.

## FROM SCOTLAND WITH LOVE

While Maytag's approach to reinventing Anchor—using quality ingredients, emphasizing tradition, avoiding growth for growth's sake, and

stubbornly clinging to staunch independence—would eventually inform craft brewing in general, it was slow going at first. The company took years to turn a profit, partly because there just wasn't much of a market for what they were selling.

That's the same problem that dogged Jack McAuliffe, who took his own shot at a craft brew revival around the same time that Maytag took over Anchor. A navy vet who'd developed a thirst for Scottish beer while on his tour of duty through Europe, McAuliffe picked up a book on homebrewing and made his own take. It turned out to be a hit not only with his fellow service-men, but among the local Scots who sampled it. Emboldened, McAuliffe returned to California after his discharge and established the New Albion Brewing Co. in Sonoma, about 45 minutes north of San Francisco.

## AMERICAN ORIGINALS

In terms of brewing, McAuliffe was hugely successful, producing an array of beers—including

what he claims was the first American pale ale, as well as a porter and a stout—that lured local customers even as he struggled to cobble together a medium-size brewing operation.

After starting New Albion with repurposed dairy equipment and soda syrup drums, McAuliffe plowed his company's cash back into an ambitious expansion plan, only to be frustrated by a dearth of suitable investors. By 1982, New Albion was bankrupt and McAuliffe was out of the beer business.

## REVOLUTION IN THE AIR

By 1970, America's five biggest breweries were responsible for half of the country's beer, a number that would continue to climb over 80 percent by the 1990s...all while the number of breweries continued to decline.

But signs of life were stirring below. During the late 1960s in Portland, Oregon, beer enthusiast Fred Eckhardt started making a name for

himself through the homebrewing classes he taught at a supply shop called Wine Art of Oregon. Perpetually needled by students to publish a book on how to make your own beer—something which, by the way, still wasn't strictly legal—in 1969 he published *Lager Beers: How to Make Good Beer at Home*. A breezy, easy-to-read breakdown of the brewing process, it weighed in at less than 50 pages and reflected a growing desire for better beer.

## GREAT AMERICAN PIONEERS

Homebrewing was finally made legal again in 1979, and while craft brewing still didn't have much market muscle, it started to build a genuine buzz. In 1982, a Boulder, Colorado, hotel played host to the inaugural Great American Beer Festival, where 30 microbreweries showed off their wares, and by the mid-1980s, a smattering of new brewers—and brewpubs—popped up on the East Coast, mirroring what initially seemed like a Western trend.

Craft brewing's story since then has been mostly onward and upward, although the industry hasn't been immune from the occasional implosion, as occurred in the late 1990s, when a third of craft brewers went out of business, the byproducts of a bubble inflated by beers produced with too much venture capital and not enough heart. But that was a corrective, not a crumbling; percentage point by percentage point, craft brewing has encroached on Big Beer's majority stake in the great American mug, to the point where, in 2014, craft's aggregate sales outpaced Budweiser for the first time in history.

It's an achievement that might sound more important than it is—we're talking about Bud alone here, not Bud Light—which means that a whole bunch of companies now combine to outsell the third most popular beer in the U.S. It's an achievement nonetheless, and indicative of how aggressively drinkers have started seeking out alternatives to the same old beer.

## NEW DAY RISING

Over a 30-year span, the number of American craft breweries surged by over 500 percent, with some of those fiercely independent breweries approaching household name status, such as Lagunitas, Brooklyn Brewery, Stone, Long Trail, and Dogfish Head, not to mention Sierra Nevada, and, still, Anchor.

But even as sales rise, craft brewing remains a community, as exemplified by this postscript. Decades after he walked away from New Albion and drifted into cult hero status among brewers, Jack McAuliffe heard from Boston Beer founder Jim Koch, who'd purchased the New Albion trademark and offered to help him resuscitate his beer by funding an initial run and giving him all the profits to fix what Koch called a "karmic imbalance." It was too little, too late for McAuliffe, who wasn't interested in brewing as a career anymore, but his daughter was. Thanks to Boston Beer's largesse, a well-preserved yeast strain, and that traditional American thirst for quality beer, the nation's original pale ale is back on the market.

# IT'S OKTOBERFEST!

• On October 12, 1810, Munich hosted the wedding of the future King Ludwig I to Princess Therese of Saxony-Hildburghausen. The public was invited to attend the festivities, held in a field outside of the city's gates. Much beer has imbibed, and everyone had so much fun that it became an annual Bavarian tradition.

• Oktoberfest is the biggest annual "people's fair" on the planet. It features rides, concerts, traditional German garb…and about 6.4 million people who consume 6.7 million liters of beer.

• Since 1810, Oktoberfest has been canceled 24 times due to decent excuses, such as wars and disease epidemics.

• *Oktober*fest is held in September. Munich's weather is better then, and the festival ends on the first Sunday in October.

# BEER BY
# THE NUMBERS

**Number of Breweries in the U.S. in 1990:** 298
**Number of Breweries in the U.S. in 2014:** 3,200

**As of 2013, the state with the most craft breweries** is California, with 381. Washington, with 201, ranks second. In third place is Oregon, with 181. Mississippi ranks dead last, with a thirst-inducing four craft breweries.

**In 2013, overall beer sales dropped by nearly two percent...** but *craft beer* sales surged by 17 percent, marking a full decade of double-digit year-to-year growth for the craft sector. That year, the overall domestic beer market hit $100 billion, $14.3 billion of which came from craft beer sales.

**The top 5 bestselling American craft breweries:** Boston Beer Company, Sierra Nevada, New Belgium, Spoetzel, and Magic Hat Brewing.

Beer-Topia

**The top 5 bestselling styles of craft beer in the United States:** Seasonal and limited editions (like winter ale and pumpkin-flavored beers); India pale ales; other pale ales; amber ales; and amber lagers.

**Biggest Beer-Drinking Countries (Per Capita)**

1. Czech Republic, 148.6 liters
2. Austria, 107.8 liters
3. Germany, 106.1 liters
4. Estonia, 102.4 liters
5. Poland, 98.5 liters
6. Ireland, 98.3 liters
7. Croatia, 85.9 liters
8. Venezuela, 85.5 liters
9. Finland, 84.2 liters
10. Romania, 83.2 liters

Where do other beer-loving countries rank? The U.S. is 14th (77.1 liters), Belgium is 18th (74 liters), the U.K. is 22nd (68.5 liters), and Canada is 25th (66.9 liters).

# A CHILD'S GARDEN OF HOPS TRIVIA

• **Hops are part of the marijuana family.**
The Cannabaceae family of flowering
plants has two genera: *Cannabis*, or marijuana, and *Humulus*. There are three species
of that, including *H. lupulus*, or brewing hops.

• **All hops are not created equal.** Brewers use
aroma hops and bittering hops to fine-tune the
flavor of their beer, and both varieties do pretty
much exactly what you'd think. But there are tons
of other varietals, like the snooty-sounding noble
hops from Europe, which are used in traditional
lagers and have names like Saaz, Hallertauer
Mittelfrüh, Tettnanger, and Spalt.

• **Hops grown in different regions have different
flavor profiles.** The Germans tend to have an
herbal flavor, the English have spicy or fruity overtones, and the Americans taste like citrus or pine.

• **Hops were first imported to the Americas by settlers during colonial times.** At one point, New York was the biggest hops producer in the U.S., but a combination of adverse conditions—including mildew and Prohibition—brought that to an end. The next boom happened in Wisconsin, where farmers turned to hops after wheat prices tanked, but that created a bubble that eventually burst, crashing the hops market. Today, roughly 80 percent of the nation's hops are grown in Washington's Yakima Valley, which means that the people bottling your favorite "locally sourced" craft brew aren't being entirely honest.

• **Only the female of the species produces the oils necessary for good drinking.** In fact, most commercial farmers remove male hops from their crop fields entirely—they're used only for pollination.

• **Hops produce *phytoestrogens,*** the plant compounds that mimic estrogen and are occasionally claimed to cause "man boobs" in men who practice excessive consumption.

Beer-Topia

• **Bitterness isn't the only thing hops impart during the brewing process,** but it is a key component of any beer's flavor. This is why we have a scale measured in International Bittering Units, or IBUs. Some brewers practice what's called "extreme hopping," loading up their beers with IBUs in the thousands—but those people are crazy, partly because after 120 IBUs or so, your taste buds can't really tell the difference.

• **Hops aren't just for beer.** As if their contribution to the flavor and preservation of such a marvelous beverage weren't enough, hops are used in all kinds of other products, including shampoos and lotions, and some companies even turn a profit by selling dried ones as decorative plants. Hops have also been used as a sleep aid (you can make a tea out of them), and the ancient Romans ate them like asparagus.

# HOW TO TALK LIKE A BREWER

*Some real terms used by real beermakers.*

**Mash.** Mixing crushed malt with hot water, thus converting grain starches to fermentable sugars. Mash is what you're left with, along with wort.

**Wort.** Before beer is beer, it's wort—the solution that results after the malt is mashed, the hops are boiled, and everything is strained. It starts off as sweet wort, then becomes brewed wort, fermenting wort, and then, finally, beer.

**Fermentation.** The magic that makes beer possible. On a chemical level, it refers to what happens while yeast converts sugars into ethyl alcohol (or "alcohol") and carbon dioxide gas (or "bubbles.")

**Lautering.** The pre-boil step of removing sweet wort from spent grains, it allows mash to settle.

Beer-Topia

**Sparge.** The stage of the brewing process in which the brewer rinses the grains with hot water in order to remove the leftover liquid malt sugar and extracts from the grain husks.

**Pitch.** The act of adding yeast to the wort after it's been allowed to cool.

**Kräeusen.** Release the kräeusen! It's the head of foam that develops on top of the wort. "Kräeusening" is also the name of a secondary fermentation technique, in which unfermented or partially fermented wort is added to a fully fermented beer.

**Alpha acids.** Resins derived from hops. During the boiling process, they're converted to iso-alpha acids, which are responsible for much of a beer's bitterness.

**Noble hops.** The distinguished title bequeathed upon several beloved strains of hops, hailing from four regions in Europe: Hallertau (Bavaria, Germany); Saaz (Zatec, Czech Republic); Spalt (Spalter, Germany); and Tettnang (Lake Constance, Germany).

**Dry hopping.** Adding dried hops to brewing beer. It takes place late in the process in order to maximize hoppy aroma without imparting bitterness.

**Wet hopping.** The act of adding freshly harvested hops to the brew before they've been dried, which gives the beer a cleaner, more vibrant flavor.

**Beta acids.** Another hop-derived acid, they preserve the brew.

**Adjunct.** A fermentable substitute for traditional grains typically added to make a beer lighter or cheaper to produce.

**All-malt.** A beer made without adjuncts.

**Priming.** Adding sugar to a maturing brew to induce secondary fermentation.

**Secondary fermentation.** Fermentation that occurs in bottles or casks over a period of weeks or months.

**Malt extract.** A syrup or powder used by brewers to reconstitute wort for fermentation, consisting of condensed wort that contains maltose, dextrins, and other dissolved solids.

**Flocculation.** How suspended particles tend to clump together during the brewing process, including yeast, proteins, and tannins.

**Trub.** A layer of sediment that collects at the bottom of the fermentation vessel. It contains heavy fats, proteins, hop oils, inactive yeast, and tannins.

**Esters.** Yet another flavor compound, esters appear during fermentation and lend beer a fruity, flowery, or spicy taste.

**Phenols.** One of many chemical compounds that make their way into the brewing process. Like a lot of them, phenols can be useful in certain amounts (smoke beers or German-style wheat beers, for instance), but don't go too far; if you let too many phenols elbow their way in, you're left with a brew that tastes like Band-Aids.

**Dextrin.** A by-product of the enzymes in the barley during fermentation, dextrin is an unfermentable carbohydrate that imparts mouthfeel, flavor, and body. Taste malt or sweetness in your beer? That's dextrin.

**Diacetyl.** A compound created during the brewing process that's said to add a butterscotch flavor to the beer. It's desirable at low levels in some beer—if you've had an English or Scottish ale, you've tasted diacetyl.

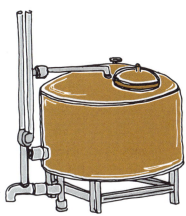

**Dimethyl sulfide (DMS).** Like diacetyl, only instead of butterscotch, the flavor is a general sweetness…except at higher levels, when it's said to taste like cooked corn or celery.

**Bung.** A wooden stopper that fills a hole in a keg or cask—the bung hole. Why don't they just call it a stopper? Well, because "bung" is more fun to say; also, it's from the Dutch word *bonghe,* or hole.

**Balling degrees.** Devised by 19th-century Czechoslovakian brewing genius C. J. N. Balling, this is a scale used to measure the density of sugars in wort, which helps determine a beer's *gravity*.

**Zymurgy.** The science of fermentation (and the name of a magazine published by the American Homebrewers Association).

# FOR YOUR HEALTH!

*Real print advertisements for beer from the early 20th century, with some very dubious health claims.*

"Every doctor knows how Beer benefits. If you need more strength or vitality, he will prescribe it. For run-down, nervous people, there is no better tonic and nutrient than a glass of good Primo Beer with meals. For well people, nothing is so conducive to good health." **(Primo Beer)**

"Beer is good, because everything in it is good. Beer is as pure as Nature and hygienic brewing can make it. It contains all the nutriment of rich malt, the tang of hops, and clear sparkling water. Nothing but the very best of these are used in beer from the breweries of your own State. Serve beer in your home at any time. Enjoy it regularly and benefit from its goodness. Drink more beer. It's good for you!" **(Resch's Beer)**

"A case of Blatz Beer in your home means much to the young mother, and obviously baby participates in its benefits. The malt in the beer supplies nourishing qualities that are essential at this time and the hops act as an appetizing, stimulating tonic." **(Blatz Beer)**

"People who drink plenty of beer are always strong and healthy. Prof. Dr. O. Bauer, Berlin, Germany, says:

'Of the 75 employees of Haase's Brewery, each of whom drinks daily over a gallon of beer, 56 have stood the rigid physical examination for enrollment in the army and are soldiers. Of the remaining 18, eight are minors, three were found too small in stature, and four were rejected for defects suffered by accident.'

Pure, well-aged beer, like Gerst Beer is a tonic, an appetizer, and a food that is nourishing and strengthening. Solid foods often remain in the stomach a long time and retard digestion. Liquid foods, like Gerst Beer, are an aid to digestion." **(Gerst Beer)**

# STRANGE BEER FLAVORS

**Frankincense and myrrh.**
Plenty of—if not most—craft breweries offer seasonal beer at Christmastime, but this is the only one that looks to the Three Wise Men for inspiration. Gift of the Magi, dreamed up by the

California-based Lost Abbey Brewery, is what the company calls "a massive Golden Ale fit for a king (or queen)"—or the King of Kings. This 9.5% ABV is made with the bark of frankincense and a hint of myrrh (no gold though).

**Marijuana.** This joint collaboration between Washington State brewers Redhook and Hilliard is a "dubious collaboration between two buds." Poured from a tap handle shaped like a bong, this beer was inspired by the legalization of marijuana in Washington, and contains hemp seeds. Sip a

glass of Joint Effort and you can expect "a dank, resinous hop aroma balanced by nutty earthiness," as well as an increased desire to play hacky sack and listen to Widespread Panic.

**Bull testicles.** You know the saying, "Why buy the cow when you can get the milk for free?" We wonder why you'd buy the beer when it's made from a recipe that calls for "25 pounds of freshly sliced and roasted bull testicles." But clearly not everyone feels that way: Weighing in at 7.5% ABV and 3 BPBs (balls per barrel), this "meaty foreign-style stout" from Wynkoop became a cult favorite in the Denver area, where it drew raves at the 2012 Great American Beer Festival and was amusingly distributed in canned two-packs. "Overall I can't say that I can taste the testicles that are brewed into this beer," reads one review, "but it's still a pretty good stout."

**Habañero.** San Diego's Ballast Point does a lot of fun stuff with their beer, emblemized by their Sculpin, a line of IPAs brewed with hops at five separate stages. Sculpin, named after a

spiny, bottom-dwelling fish, comes in more than one eyebrow-raising flavor—you can also get it in Grapefruit—but the boldest of them all is Habañero, which adds an extra layer of heat to IPA's traditional citrusy hops.

**Pickle.** Any weird beer enthusiast worth his suds will eventually delve into the American wild ale, a variety brewed using nontraditional yeasts and one whose overriding flavor characteristic is often described as "funky." That's as good a starting point as any for discussion of Slippery Pig's Pickle Sour, which holds true to the Washington-based brewery's M.O. They stick to local ingredients for their beer, including pickles. It definitely isn't something you'd want to serve to your Bud Light–loving friends, but if ever there was a beer you'd want to use for fried pickle batter at the state fair, this is it.

**Pizza.** Pizza and beer have been best friends for decades, so why not stuff 'em together in the same bottle? Brewers Tom and Athena Seefurth use a recipe that includes "a surplus of tomatoes, a bag

Beer-Topia

of garlic, and an idea." Unlike some oddly flavored brews that use only a dash of this or that weird ingredient, Mamma Mia! Pizza Beer goes all in: The brewing process includes a margarita pizza that's dropped into the mash and "steeped like a tea bag."

**Crème brûlée.** Beer for dessert? Hey, why not? Southern Tier Brewery of New Jersey makes this treat. Proof that a beer can pack a wallop (this one weighs in at 9.6% ABV) and still be surprisingly sweet, this imperial milk stout lives up to its name with a scent and flavor that has more in common with custard than it probably has any right to. And yet it balances all that sugary goodness with plenty of old-fashioned stouty heft.

**Algae.** If you've ever been to a smoothie stand or set foot in a health-food shop, you've probably heard of spirulina, a blue-green algae that the Aztecs ate hundreds of years before it became a trendy "superfood" additive for people who enjoy stuffing their meals and beverages with added vitamins…or people who feel like giving a

sweet-smelling, green-tinted beer a whirl. A seasonal brew that tends to surface at the tap around St. Patrick's Day (get it?), Freetail's Spirulina Wit may not be quite as healthy as a glass full of yogurt and kale, but if you're looking to replenish your electrolytes after running a few miles or a round of racquetball, it's probably better than a Gatorade.

**Beard.** A litmus test for the level of weirdness a beer drinker is willing to tolerate, Rogue's Beard beer is brewed using yeast grown in strands of master brewer John Maier's facial hair. This isn't quite as gross as it may sound—it isn't as though you're going to take a deep swig and end up picking something curly out from between your teeth. Still, while it's definitely weird in concept, it also reflects Rogue's belief in brewing using homegrown stuff; they harvest their own barley and hops, and they turned to Maier's beard during a lengthy search for an exclusive yeast.

**Scorpions.** Aside from packing an eyebrow-raising list of ingredients, this imperial Mexican-style lager

Beer-Topia

from Charlotte's Unknown Brewing Company also boasts what might be the longest name of any beer on the market: La Jordana del Escorpion en Fuego Hacia la Casa del Chupacabra Muerto, which translates to "The Path of the Fiery Scorpion through the House of the Dead Chupacabra." As you might suspect, this brew isn't messing around: Its 10.1% ABV is the end result of a brewing process that includes agave nectar and serrano peppers, aging on tequila oak staves—and 99 scorpions. Asked what that could possibly do for the beer's flavor, head brewer Brad Shell shrugged and offered the best possible answer, saying, "I'm not sure, that's not the point. The point is this beer needs scorpions. Some things just have to happen."

SKIP THE CHEAP STUFF

DRINK
*Good*
BEER

# TOTALLY NECESSARY BEER GADGETS

**Gadget:** eCool

**What it Does:** Developed by a group of geniuses from Mors, an island in northern Denmark, the eCool is a subterranean Rube Goldberg–style cooler. It uses a long paddle wheel rigged up to a handle in order to store beer underground, keeping it perfectly chilled year-round without the aid of electricity, ice, or toxic coolants. Any time you want a beer, just pop off the lid, turn the handle, and grab a brew; add a new one to replace the one you took, and repeat as necessary.

Getting it set up requires some manual labor (the eCool website says "it's advised to use a garden drill, but can be installed with a shovel as well, if you're a real man"), but that just gives you an excuse to drink up the burned calories.

**Gadget:** The Chillsner
**What it Does:** You've probably experienced the bitter disappointment of finishing a beer after it's gotten a little too warm. Enter the Chillsner, a slender cooling tube (stainless steel on the outside, space-age gel on the inside) that drops into your bottle and keeps room temperature at bay. It even attaches to its own lid, meaning you don't have to fish around in your empty bottle to get it out. And the lid has vents, so you don't even have to take it out to enjoy your brew.

**Gadget:** The Growler Saver
**What it Does:** Growlers are great for bringing beer home from your local brewery, but they aren't so hot when it comes to storage—opening one accelerates the inexorable decarbonation process. There are all kinds of solutions to this problem, including a whole line of space-age, airtight jugs that will set you back hundreds of dollars. But if you want to spend a little less, you can order a Growler Saver: a cap with a built-in

nozzle for periodically injecting enough $CO_2$ to keep your beer good and fizzy indefinitely.

**Gadget:** BeerBug
**What it Does:** The BeerBug is the first in what will likely be a wave of "smart" gadgets designed to make life simpler for the home brewer. Essentially a fermentation babysitter with Wi-Fi or Bluetooth capability built in, it monitors a whole bunch of stuff about your brew, including temperature and alcohol content, and reports back to you via text or email.

**Gadget:** The GrabOpener
**What it Does:** There are a million bottle openers out there, and although none of them has ever really improved on the elegance of this timeless gadget's simple design, a few do make decent conversation starters (like the ones built into the bottom of a glass or the back of an iPhone

case) or make opening a bottle possible under less-than-ideal circumstances. Take, for example, the GrabOpener, a sharp-looking doohickey that uses leverage to let you open a bottle with one hand. Brace the neck with your thumb, hook the GrabOpener to the cap, push down on the other end with your fingers, and voilà!

**Gadget:** Randall the Enamel Animal
**What it Does:** This $300 device is less "gadget" than "lifestyle decision"—it's a beer infuser that makes adding flavors to your brew as simple as packing a couple of chambers.

**Gadget:** Bottoms Up
**What it Does:** While pouring beer isn't exactly difficult, doing it correctly is the kind of thing that requires a little bit of patience, knowledge, and dexterity. But what if you

could pour beer into your glass from the bottom? Bottoms Up Beer has developed technology that relies on a magnet system to temporarily unlock a hole in the bottom of the glass and deliver a perfect pour. And although the company's systems are all pretty pricey, with the cheapest model starting at $1,500, they're easily incredible enough to justify the cost. And they aren't even finished: The Bottoms Up line is expanding to include an easy chair with beer-filling technology built into the seat.

**Gadget:** Drop Shots

**What it Does:** There are a handful of cocktails out there—okay, we can only think of two, the Boilermaker and the Irish Car Bomb—that involve plunging a shotglass of a spirit into a pint of beer. One is meant to drink the whole thing bottoms up, but when bottoms are up, the shot glass has a tendency to fall out onto the drinker's face. The solution: Drop Shots. It's a pint and shotglass set, and the shotglass stays put inside the pint glass with…magnets.

# 83 FUNNY CRAFT BEER NAMES

Peter Cotton Ale

Dead Guy Ale

Hoptimus Prime

Yippie Rye Aye

Audrey Hopburn

Josef Bierbitzch
("get me a Bierbitzch")

Stop, Hop and Roll

Monty Python's
Holy Ale

Over Hopulation

Polygamy Porter

Fermentation Without
Representation

Alimony Ale
("the bitterest beer in
America")

Java the Nut

Delerium Tremens

Old Leghumper

Honey Boo Brew

The Big Lebrewski

Me, My Spelt,
and Rye

Brew Free or Die IPA

Peter Piper's Pickled
Pepper Purple Peated
Pale Ale

Pumpkin Brewster

Smooth Hoperator

Moose Drool

He'Brew:
The Chosen Beer

Genghis Pecan

For Those About
to Bock

Blithering Idiot

Vergina

Old Engine Oil

Spleen Cleaver

Ill-Tempered Gnome

Men's Room Red

Spicy Fish Wife

Buckin' Monk

Dog's Bollocks

Kilt Lifter

Irish Death

Arrogant Bastard Ale

Face Plant

Yeastus Christ

Moo Thunder Stout

Porkslap Pale Ale

Buttface Amber Ale

Yellow Snow

Soft Dookie

Bishop's Finger

Ryan and the
Beaster Bunny

Tactical Nuclear
Penguin

Judas Yeast

Santa's Butt Porter

Seriously Bad Elf

I'll Have What the
Gentleman on the
Floor Is Having

Screaming Ape Porter

Black Metal

Apocalypse Cow

Vas Deferens

Wreck the Halls

Farmer's Tan

Mama's Little
Yellow Pils

400 Pound Monkey

Beer-Topia

Panty Peeler

Rigor Mortis

Meat Whistle

Human Blockhead

Wake Up Dead

Mash of the Titans

Doctor Morton's
Clown Poison

Gandhi-Bot

Little Sumpin' Sumpin'

Hoppy Ending

Overrated
West Coast IPA

Ninja vs. Unicorn

Sweaty Betty

Scotland Charred

Big Falcon Deal

Those Candies Your
Granny Loves
Brown Ale

Vampire Blood

Hell or High
Watermelon

Pandora's Bock

Nonethewizer

You Will Fail Ale

Larry Bird's Haircut

Standard Issue IPA

Drink
UP

# A GUIDE TO LAGERS

SOME CALL ME
THE
*Lager*
MAN

PINT ME    ASAP

**Pilsner.** It arrived on the scene relatively late, first appearing in 1842, but pilsner has made up for lost time, quickly rising to enjoy worldwide beer supremacy (at least in terms of market share). It isn't hard to understand why: With its clean, simple flavor and low bitterness, pilsner is a refreshing, easy drink that goes well with just about everything. Like Xerox or Band-Aids, "Pilsner" started out as the name of a specific brew, Pilsner Urquell, before being unfurled as a global umbrella that covers everything from its assorted Czech and German varieties to American pale lagers like Budweiser, Coors, and Rolling Rock.

**Bock.** A stronger lager, bock tends to be darker and maltier than its cousins. Traditionally smooth

Beer-Topia

with lower carbonation and negligible hop flavor, it's also brewed in the lighter, hoppier malbock or helles bock style, as well as the stronger doppelbock, which bears the distinction of being the original "liquid bread"—a drink used for sustenance by fasting friars. Finally, there's the eisbock, which is sort of the Bud Ice of traditional German beer: a doppelbock that's partially frozen during the brewing process, and emerges as a more flavorful (and alcoholic) brew after the ice is scooped out. This style's name (and the goat that appears on some labels) comes from its origins as an ale brewed in Einbeck during the 14th century. When the recipe was adapted as a lager by Munich brewers hundreds of years later, they pronounced Einbeck as "ein bock," or "a billy goat."

**Märzen.** This is a style with its roots in Bavaria, where, starting in the 16th century, brewers could only make beer between September and April. Barrels of Märzen—described in its original incarnation as "dark brown, full-bodied, and bitter"—were stored in cellars throughout

the rest of the year, with leftover barrels served during the traditional Oktoberfest celebration (hence Märzen's current interchangeable status with "Oktoberfest"-style brews). The modern Märzen varies in color, although the Austrian varieties tend to be lighter and sweeter than their German counterparts.

**Dunkel.** Sort of the lager version of a porter, the dunkel is championed by the German Beer Institute as "the world's first true beer style"; the merits of this claim may be debatable, but the dunkel's appeal as a full-bodied dark brew with a clean lager finish is hard to dispute. The dunkel family also includes dunkelweizen, a dark wheat beer.

# SOMETHING IN THE WATER

Beer snobs talk a lot about which types of hops were used to make a brew, or what kind of malt went into it. But many of us don't really think about the water—even though it makes up 90 percent of any given beer. But with so many craft brews being produced across the nation, where the quality and makeup of water resources vary greatly, it's got to account for something. It's important to recognize how crucial $H_2O$ really is to the flavor (and more) of a beer.

Like everything else in brewing, there's a science to water and beer. The profile of the water used—taking into account the variety and amounts of minerals, as well as its pH—can have a major impact. The main components a brewer looks at are carbonate, sodium, chloride, sulfate, calcium, and magnesium.

As for home brewing, those who take it seriously get a local water analysis before they begin the process. Among the cities with water that has a good balance of those minerals, and a near-perfect pH: Antwerp, Belgium; Munich, Germany; and Denver, Colorado. It's no coincidence that those three places are among the most renowned and celebrated beer capitals. And if the water in your city rates poorly, your brew supply store sells plenty of tools to get your water more in line with optimum brewing conditions. Sometimes it's as easy as simple additives like salt, gypsum, or baking soda.

All of this might sound a little daunting if you're just starting out and trying to sort your wort from your mash, but don't worry. Even if your local water doesn't have the mystical qualities imparted to your favorite craft brew, it has plenty of other stuff all its own. Just like the hops, malt, and yeast, it's a unique ingredient, and one that, over time, the savvy brewer learns to use to his or her advantage.

# THE BEER BELLY: FACT OR FICTION?

Of all the stereotypes that go along with beer drinkers, the beer belly might be the most widespread. Think of a prototypical beer drinker. Did you think of Norm from *Cheers*? You probably did. But has beer been given a bad rap as the cause of male belly fat?

Well, yes and no. While it's true that beer has a moderate to high amount of calories, there's nothing about this particular beverage that sends those calories straight to your gut. Just like doing sit-ups won't magically make your belly fat disappear, beer won't head straight for your spare tire. The caloric content in beer varies widely, but the average is somewhere in the neighborhood of 150 calories per 12 ounces. If you watch your diet at all, you'll be able to see what that means for you in terms of your daily allowance, and how quickly those numbers add up.

But it isn't just the calories that work against your svelte figure. It's also the alcohol, which jumps to the front of the line when it hits your metabolic system. While your liver is tied up purging it, any food you've recently eaten has to wait to be broken down, and it ends up being stored as fat...generally in the belly area.

Lifestyle is also a factor. Moderate drinkers are apt to be more diet-conscious and adjust their caloric intake (or exercise) to offset their imbibing. Heavy beer drinkers, on the other hand, tend to be more sedentary, and to have less healthy habits in general. In short, beer is more of symptom than a cause.

And if you don't drink a lot or eat a lot of junk, but still find yourself getting soft in the middle, that might be due to age and genetics. Most of us acquire some extra padding as we get older, and we all add our padding differently. It could be that your "beer belly" has more to do with DNA than IPA.

# BEER UNDER PROHIBITION

President Herbert Hoover called it "a noble experiment," but today, most Americans remember Prohibition (1920–1933) as a *failed* experiment. In an effort to enforce temperance by criminalizing the manufacture, sale, and transport of "intoxicating liquor," the government ended up sparking a huge increase in illegal activity instead, notably the rise of organized crime in the United States.

Breweries shed thousands of jobs during Prohibition, but surprisingly, they didn't die out entirely. They branched out into other areas. Yuengling and Anheuser-Busch delved into ice cream as a way to utilize their expensive fleets of refrigerated trucks. Yuengling's ice

cream proved so popular, in fact, that the company kept on producing it into the 1980s. Coors, meanwhile, expanded its pottery and glassworks divisions (really) and produced a line of family dinnerware.

The big breweries made near beer, too. "Popular" brands included Pablo by Pabst, Famo by Schlitz, Vivo by Miller, Lux-O by Stroh, and Bevo by Anheuser-Busch, but consumers wanted stronger stuff. The industry was still happy to oblige, by implicitly encouraging homebrewing through the sale of malt extract.

It was advertised as a baking aid, but this was a ruse and everyone knew it; as Prohibition agent A.W. McDaniel wrote sarcastically at the time, "There is an enormous amount of baking done, according to the amount of extracts being sold." The government initially tried to stop the production of malt extract, but brewers successfully lobbied to have it classified as food, and it stayed on the market, where it did increasingly well; in 1927,

for example, 450 million pounds of the stuff were produced. Sales of near beer subsequently plummeted. By 1929, homebrewers were churning out 700 million gallons annually.

That's an impressive figure, but the brews themselves were generally pretty dismal. Forced to do it all on the sly, homebrewers were often left with sludgy beer that was preferable only to no beer at all. Muddy, sour, and occasionally combustible, they were dismissed by the secretary of the U.S. Brewers Association as a "poor imitation of old-fashioned stock ales."

Once drinkers could get the real thing, on the other hand, they were just as willing to abandon homebrewing. In fact, it quickly dropped out of vogue after Prohibition's repeal and didn't even officially become legal in the U.S. until 1979.

# HOW TO OPEN A BEER WITHOUT A BOTTLE OPENER

*We are not responsible if you hurt yourself, but please be careful anyway.*

**With a dollar bill.** Fold a dollar bill in half, and then roll it up incredibly tight to where it's about half an inch wide. Fold this very stiff wedge of paper money and jam it under the lid, with the rolled part of the bill held between your thumb and index finger. Hold onto the neck of the bottle with your other hand, and push up and against the folded dollar. The cap should come off.

**With a lighter.** Take a disposable, flat-bottomed plastic lighter, flip it over, and place the edge of the bottom just under the beer cap's ridge. Hold the neck of the bottle tightly and push it up against the lighter. Continue doing this around the cap, five or six times, until it pops off.

**With a key.** Hold the neck of the beer bottle with your nondominant hand, and place any regular door key under the ridge of the cap with your other hand. Use the key to pry up the cap in a few spots until you've created a gap big enough to shove in the key. Finish the job by popping the cap off.

**With another beer.** A sharp or rigid piece of metal seems to be perfect for prying off a beer bottle cap, which is itself a sharp or rigid piece of metal. That means you can use one beer bottle to open another beer bottle. Take the cap of a sealed bottle and place it just under the ridge of the other bottle's cap. Jerk down on the topmost bottle and the cap should pop off.

**With a wooden spoon.** Wrap your hand around the neck, leaving just a hint of space between your hand and the ridge of the cap. Take the back end of the spoon and hook it just under the cap and pry it off. (This method keeps the cap from being bent, so use this one if you're a cap collector.)

# A TOAST TO ANDRE THE GIANT

"As far as great drunkards go, there is Andre the Giant, and then there is everyone else," wrote Richard English in *Modern Drunkard* about the professional wrestler and actor. He was a beer enthusiast whose bottomless thirst only had a little to do with his 7'4", 500-pound frame—consuming as much beer as possible was partially a party trick, and partially a way to numb the physical pain from his wrestling career.

• His favorite beer was the unpretentious Molson Canadian. (There's a widely circulated picture of Andre palming a can of it.) He drank an average of about two cases every day—that's **48 beers.** Half of those he'd drink before wrestling matches.

• On a night out drinking in Manhattan in 1977, Andre drank **75 beers.** His friends couldn't convince him to take a taxi to his hotel, which he

Beer-Topia

hated because he didn't like squeezing himself into them…so they stole a horse carriage. Andre safely returned to his hotel…bar, where he drank a gallon or so of brandy.

• He once drained **119 bottles of beer** in a six-hour drinking session, then passed out in a hotel hallway. His friends couldn't move him, so they placed a piano cover over him while he slept it off.

• Wrestling cohort Harley Race claims to have once gone out with Andre for a night of drinking in New Orleans, where he says Andre put away **127 beers.**

• Wrestlers Mike Graham, Dusty Rhodes, and Michael Hayes swear that they once witnessed Andre drink **156 bottles of beer** in a row.

• Andre's beer tab at his hotel when *The Princess Bride* finished filming: $40,000.

# 44 HOPS VARIETIES WITH COOL NAMES

*Hops give beer character, and their names reflect that.*

| | |
|---|---|
| Zeus | Sorachi Ace |
| Vanguard | Warrior |
| Topaz | Pacific Jade |
| Super Pride | Super Galena |
| Challenger | Liberty |
| Fuggle | Crystal |
| Magnum | Herkules |
| Northdown | Orbit |
| El Dorado | Tomahawk |

| | |
|---|---|
| San Juan Ruby Red | Galaxy |
| Pride of Ringwood | Palisade |
| Green Bullet | Millennium |
| Taurus | Golding |
| Southern Cross | Nugget |
| Phoenix | Sterling |
| Summit | Ultra |
| Mosaic | Glacier |
| Super Alpha | Cluster |
| Calypso | Sun |
| Sovereign | Bravo |
| Brewer's Gold | Olympic |
| Feux-Coeur Francais | Zythos |

# THE WORLD'S MOST EXPENSIVE BEERS

**Beer:** The End of History
**Price:** $765
**Story:** Dreamed up at Scotland's BrewDog, this blond Belgian ale packs an eye-watering wallop: At 55% ABV, it's one of the strongest beers on the planet. Its bottle also functions as a conversation piece, albeit a gross one: Each EOH bottle is placed inside the body of a taxidermied roadkill victim. The pricetag is justified by its scarcity—only a dozen 330 mL bottles were produced. Whether it's worth the investment is up to you, but it does boast an impressive 88 out of 100 at RateBeer.com…as well as an odor that reminded one drinker of "dog biscuit, soy, leather, Asian mushrooms, beef, and sweet chocolate," and a taste that, according to another, bears hints of "mushrooms, soy sauce, beef, leather, cherry, and tobacco."

**Beer:** Space Barley
**Price:** $110
**Story:** This beer from Sapporo is exactly what it sounds like: beer made from barley that was grown in space. Announced in 2008 and sold through a special lottery system in Japan the following year, this exceedingly limited edition produced only 250 six-packs, each of which went for more than the equivalent of a hundred bucks. That's a hefty price tag for a beer that probably didn't end up tasting all that different from one whose ingredients were harvested here on Earth, but Sapporo at least donated Space Barley profits to Okayama University to subsidize and encourage science education.

**Beer:** Crown Ambassador Reserve
**Price:** $90
**Story:** Down Under, well-heeled drinkers indulge in Crown Ambassador Reserve, a 10.2% ABV doppelbock that's periodically issued in special 8,000-bottle batches. Everything about this beer is supposed to scream "class," from its year-long

aging process in French oak barrels to the bottle, which is shaped and packaged to look like champagne. At that price for each 750 ml, it definitely isn't the kind of thing you want to be mindlessly guzzling during the game.

**Beer:** Tutankhamun Ale
**Price:** $7,600 (or $200)
**Story:** Dreamed up after an archaeologist unearthed brewing chambers used during Egyptian queen Nefertiti's reign, and brewed using a recipe extrapolated from ancient beer residue inside the chambers, Tutankhamun Ale made its debut with a 1,000-bottle run, the first of which fetched an absurd $7,686. Even at those prices, the brewery couldn't manage to stay in business, and today you can periodically find Tutankhamun on auction sites for under $200.

*For some more beers we hope you can someday afford, turn to page 133.*

# WHO OWNS WHAT

*Even though American beer fans can enjoy a vast array of craft beers, the market is still controlled by a small handful of major corporations.*

**AB InBev.** In 2008 Belgium's InBev purchased Anheuser-Busch for $52 billion, creating AB InBev. InBev itself was formed when Brazilian brewer Companhia de Bebidas merged with Belgium's Interbrew in 2004. Interbrew came about in 1987 when Brasseries Artois (brewer of Stella Artois) and Piedboeuf (maker of Jupiler) joined together. Anheuser-Busch, meanwhile, started out in St. Louis in 1860, eventually growing to dominate the American market with its line of Budweiser beers. The end result is not only the leading global brewer, but one of the world's most powerful consumer brands.

***Other AB InBev brands:*** Hoegaarden, Leffe, Skol, Kokanee, Labatt, Beck's, Löwenbräu, Spaten,

St. Pauli Girl, Bass, Boddingtons, Busch, Goose Island, Michelob, Land Shark, Natural, Rolling Rock, Shock Top, and Corona. AB InBev also has ownership stakes in many popular craft brewers, including 10 Barrel, Red Hook, Omission, Kona, and Widmer Brothers.

**Carlsberg.** In the United States, Carlsberg is little known, but in Europe, it's a powerhouse. In Russia, its Baltika controls 40 percent of the beer market. Elsewhere, their flagship Carlsberg brew is a favorite for many drinkers, and they're also heavily active throughout western, northern, and eastern Europe, as well as China, where their major stake in Chongqing Brewery gives them a foothold against the hugely popular CR Snow. In all, the Danish company produces more than 350 different beer brands.

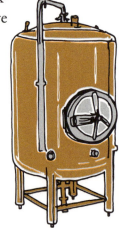

*Other Carlsberg brands:* Kronenbourg, Somersby, Jacobsen, Semper Ardens, Falcon, Ringnes, Holsten, Lübzer, Feldschlosschen, Cardinal, Super Bock, Warteck, Birrificio Angelo, Grimbergen, and Euro Beer.

**Heineken.** Heineken dates to 1864, when Gerard Adriaan Heineken purchased a tottering Amsterdam brewery called the Haystack. It's risen to span the globe as one of the few truly internationally recognizable beer brands. While Europe accounts for roughly half of its sales, Heineken drinkers (and Heineken ad campaigns) are everywhere, and the company owns more than 100 breweries in over 70 countries.

*Other Heineken brands:* Amstel, Furstenberg, Tecate, Newcastle, Sol, Kingfisher, Murphy's, Dos Equis, Strongbow, and Bohemia.

**SABMiller.** SABMiller was formed in 2002, when South African Breweries gobbled up the Miller Brewing Company, which at the time enjoyed

the second-largest market share in the U.S. The resulting partnership bridged hundreds of years of mass-market brewing tradition across either side of the Atlantic: SAB got its start in 1895 when a Swedish brewer created Castle Lager to capture the market of European miners working in Johannesburg. Miller got its start in the 1850s in Milwaukee. The chain got even more complicated in 2008, when Miller bought Molson Coors (already a merger of two famous brands) to create MillerCoors.

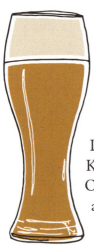

**Other SABMiller brands:** All Coors, Miller, and Molson styles (of course), Molson Killian's, Blue Moon, Pilsner Urquell, Carling, Peroni, Snow, Grolsch, Batch 19, Keystone, Henry Weinhard, Leinenkugel, Hamm's, Icehouse, Keystone, Mickey's, Milwaukee's Best, Olde English, Red Dog, Steel Reserve, and Foster's.

# HAIR OF THE DOG

*The world's scientists have yet to provide
a foolproof way of curing the hangover.
Until then: folk remedies.*

**Fried canary.** Pliny the Elder may or may not have discovered hops, which may or may not make him the grandfather of beer. His knack for throwing together a hangover cure wasn't anywhere near as sharp as his botanical aptitude—he recommended eating a fried canary to get over those morning-after blues.

**Pickled herring.** Woe to those who overindulge in Germany, because there's a distinct possibility that some well-meaning friend will serve them a plate of *katerfrühstück*, which is as harsh and intimidating as it sounds. It translates to "hangover breakfast," and for some reason, the Germans believe that means raw, pickled herring with pickle and onion bits on the side.

**Hair of the dog.** There's some legitimate science behind the idea of a morning-after Bloody Mary. Because your hangover is at its worst about 12 hours after you started drinking—or when your blood-alcohol content dips back down around zero—a low-alcohol beverage can act as a buffer.

**Lemon armpit.** We're going to tell you right up front that there seems to be little more than anecdotal evidence to suggest that anyone has actually done this. Apparently it's a custom in Puerto Rico to kick off a night of drinking by stuffing a lemon wedge in one's armpit, said to ward off dehydration.

**Rabbit poop.** In the Wild West, cowboys had to make do with what they had on hand, which explains two things: 1) why they were often forced to indulge in rotgut booze that would just as soon kill you as make you drunk; and 2) why they tended to cope with the pain that came with the morning after by brewing up a tea steeped with rabbit droppings.

**Pickle juice.** There's a lot of pickled stuff on this list, and for good reason: All those spices and salt and pickled ingredients pack a big load of the electrolytes that can help you get back on the good foot when your head is pounding and your mouth feels like it's been stuffed full of cotton.

**Bull penis.** Sicilians know how to party, apparently—one of their favorite time-tested hangover remedies is to sit and gnaw for a while on dried bull's genitals. We can't imagine that it actually helps soothe the pain, but it at least gives you something extra-pungent to remember the next time you think about having a potentially disastrous "one last drink."

**Tomato juice and eyeballs.** On second thought, dried bull penis sounds pretty fantastic compared to the foul cocktail Mongolians throw together when they want to dry out: tomato juice and pickled sheep's eyes.

# BETTER LIVING THROUGH PACKAGING

In the Olden Days, beer drinkers had to lug their suds home in growler buckets or refillable bottles made out of stoneware. Prefilled cans and bottles are comparatively miraculous, but we might not yet have reached the pinnacle of beer container technology. Here are a few recent innovations.

**PET bottles.** For years, cans were the cooler, newer alternative to bottles—and then for years after that, they were seen as the bottle's trashy cousin. These days, there's a lively debate over whether beer tastes better from a bottle or a can, but before long, we could get another alternative: PET bottles, which, despite their name, are unfortunately not containers shaped like dogs or cats. PET (*polyethylene terephthalate*) is a recyclable plastic that's lighter than glass, making it eco-friendly on both legs of its journey to and from consumers. It also uses "gas-barrier technology"

to give the beer inside a six-month shelf life. Economically and environmentally, PET bottles could be a boon for brewers, but the true test will be with consumers; after years of being conditioned to believe beer should stay far away from plastic, convincing drinkers of its benefits will likely be an uphill battle.

**Topless cans.** Not a variation on the NSFW packaging used by Nude Beer (see page 27), but an idea introduced by Pennsylvania craft brewery Sly Fox, which uses a pull tab connected to a lid that lifts right off the beer. Cleverly engineered to prevent sharp edges, it gives the drinker the full-flavor, aromatic experience you'd get out of a glass, but eliminates the need to pour it anywhere but straight down your gullet. The topless can hasn't exactly taken the beer industry by storm since being introduced in 2013; as of this writing, Sly Fox is the only brewer using it.

**"Cold-activated" packaging.** MillerCoors is quite proud of its Innovation department, although

projects like the pour-enhancing "Vortex bottle" bear the distinct odor of empty hype. One area where we have to hand it to them, however, is their line of "cold-activated" beer, which comes in packaging that changes appearance when the beer reaches optimal drinking temperature. With the cold-activated window pack, you can tell whether your case of Coors Light is sufficiently chilled; with individually cold-activated bottles and cans, you can just wait for the Rockies on the label to turn blue. With the newer two-stage cold activation packaging, the label sports a "Super Cold" activation bar.

**The "Ignite" bottle.** If you're the type of drinker who pines for a *Jetsons*-style future in which every last component of our lives is somehow "interactive," you'll enjoy Heineken's prototype "Ignite" bottle. Loaded with accelerometers and with WiFi capability, the bottle is programmed to give drinkers a light show when they take a swig, say "cheers," or happen to be sitting in a venue where the DJ has been handed the digital keys to make

Beer-Topia

everyone's Heineken join the party. The presumably high price tag (and, frankly, the annoyance of a light-up beer bottle) seems likely to keep this in the concept stage for a while, but it may not be long before you see the "Ignite" at special bar events.

**Grolsch's Mason jar.** Grolsch, which has made a name for itself with its resealable hinged bottles, recently test-marketed the "Borcanul" container in Romania. It's a sealed jar with a handle on it.

**Bottlecap movie tickets.** Also courtesy of Grolsch, this rather odd (yet ultimately fairly useful) idea tucks a Bluetooth sensor onto the underside of your bottlecap, which turns on after being opened and unlocks access to consumer content. Initially used in conjunction with a service called Movie Unlocker (which does pretty much exactly what it sounds like), the technology would seem to have widespread implications, particularly for promotional tie-ins allowing brewers to lure drinkers with promises of free stuff.

# THE UNIVERSAL LANGUAGE

*Or how to ask for a "beer" all around the world.*

**Afrikaans:** Bier

**Spanish:** Cerveza

**Basque:** Garagardoa

**Filipino:** Serbesa

**Esperanto:** Biero

**Danish:** Øl

**Cantonese:** Pear zao

**Mandarin:** Pi jiu

**Amharic:** Bira

**Hungarian:** Sör

**Armenian:** Garejure

**Khmer:** Dughck

**Somalian:** Khamri

**Welsh:** Cwrw

**Gaelic:** Leann

**Estonian:** Kesvamärjuke

**Belarusian:** Piva

**Czech:** Pivo

**Finnish:** Olut

**Manx:** Lhuner

**Luganda:** Bbiya

**Navajo:** Hólóní

**Greenlandic:** Immaaraq

**Tamil:** Madhubaanam

**Japanese:** Biiru

**Latin:** Fermentum

**Farsi:** Ab'jo

**Polish:** Piwo

**Korean:** Mek-ju

**Lakota:** M'nee-pee-gah

**Punjabi:** Bir sharab

**Lithuanian:** Alu

**Nepali:** Jad

**Arabic:** Beereh

**Icelandic:** Bjór

**Xhosa:** Ibhiye

**Romanian:** Bere

**Zulu:** Utshwala

*Beer-Topia*

# BEER TREATS

*What beer drinkers eat when
they're not drinking beer.*

**Beer-flavored coffee.** Even if you're the type of coffee drinker who thinks Starbucks overcharges for sugary, burned coffee drinks, you'd probably be interested in its Dark Barrel Latte, a drink the chain test-marketed in 2014. It consists of espresso, whipped cream, caramel, and chocolate stout-flavored syrup. It reportedly tastes a lot like a Guinness.

**Beer jelly beans.** David Klein, the founder of Jelly Belly, broke the flavor game wide open for jelly beans. His company now offers hundreds of flavors, including beer. In 2014, it debuted a Draft Beer bean. Inspired by hefeweizen and brought to market after three years of tinkering and research, it promises an "effervescent and crisp" (and alcohol-free) munching experience. Jelly Belly even

published instructions for making beer jelly bean "cocktails." Apple Cider Shandy is two parts Draft Beer, one part Red Apple, and Michelada is two parts Draft Beer, one part Lemon-Lime, and one part Tabasco.

**Beer and pretzel caramels.** Some insane flavor wizard found a way to not only combine the incredibly complementary tastes of beer and pretzels into a single item, but also turn them into a delicious, gooey caramel snack. Even better, the beer in question comes from Brooklyn Brewery, whose Brown Ale and East India IPA goes into these Liddabit caramels.

**Beer brittle.** Beer and nuts go together like hops and malt. Just ask Annette's Chocolates in Napa, California, where they've concocted a fabulous line of beer brittle that includes a microbrew

Beer-Topia

recipe (Spanish peanuts, ale, brittle, and salt) as well as a "fiery" option that includes hot peppers.

**Beer candy.** At Beercandy.com, shoppers can choose from three options: Beercandy caramels (made with stout, IPA, and lager), Beertaffy (IPA and stout), or Hopdrops ("a surprising marriage of bitter and sweet").

**Beer potato chips.** Kettle-cooked and beer-flavored. Goodness gracious, people, what more do you want in a potato chip? Made by Sprecher, these are only available in the Milwaukee area (or online).

**Beer ice cream.** Frozen Pints' beer-flavored ice creams do provide a bit of a buzz, and it comes in a variety of beer flavors, including Honey IPA, Vanilla Bock, and Pumpkin Ale. It's frozen, so you can't order online. You can only get a scoop at a Frozen Pints store in Georgia. (Make a beer pilgrimage out of it—there's a store just down the road from the Billy Carter Museum in Plains.)

# THE UNITED STATES OF BEER, PART 1

**Alabama:** Craft brewing exploded in the Yellowhammer State in 2009, when the Gourmet Beer Bill went into effect, allowing the legal alcohol volume limit in local beer to increase from 6 percent to 13.9 percent. One of the biggest breweries to emerge from Alabama is Good People Brewing Company. Known for using a seven-barrel brewing system, GP produces a robust lineup that includes a brown ale, pale ale, several IPAs, a chocolate oatmeal stout, and its Snake Handler Double IPA.

**Alaska:** Alaskan Brewing Company is one of the nation's oldest craft brewers. Founded in 1986, it's the first brewer to set up in Juneau since Prohibition. That pioneering opened the door to competition like Midnight Sun Brewing Company, whose lineup includes Monk's Mistress Belgian Strong Dark Ale, a hefty brew weighing in at 11.5% ABV.

Beer-Topia

**Arizona:** In 2014, users at RateBeer.com voted Gilbert-based Arizona Wilderness Brewing Company the top new brewery in the *world*. Its evolving lineup includes everything from sour wheat ale to porter and IPA options, and a cockeyed sense of humor evident in the slogan "handcrafted beer, facecrafted beards."

**Arkansas:** In 2010, there were only four craft breweries in Arkansas. Today, there are 20, impressive considering most are outgrowths of part-time garage-brewing hobbyists, and also because alcohol is illegal in half of the state's counties. A standout: Core Brewing in Springdale, and its flagship ESB.

**California:** A beer lover could easily take a two-week beer tour of California, where craft brewers give the state's famous wineries some real competition. But if we had to settle

on just one brewery to visit in the entire state, it'd have to be the place where the craft brewing explosion really started: San Francisco's Anchor Brewing Company. Founded in 1896 but tottering on the verge of closure by the 1960s, Anchor Steam was purchased for a few thousand dollars by Frederick Louis "Fritz" Maytag III, who came to brewing with the passion of a novice and the money to turn the company around. Purveyors of California common beer, made by brewing lager yeasts at higher temperatures, Anchor Steam left its lineup substantially unchanged for decades, but in recent years, they've introduced a number of new additions, including a brown ale, a straight lager, a barrel ale, and an IPA.

**Colorado:** The Centennial State is a craft brewing powerhouse, with places like Breckenridge Brewing, Great Divide, Left Hand, and the Oskar Blues Brewery, which helped make canned beer cool again. And then there's New Belgium Brewing Company, founded in Fort Collins in 1991. The company's flagship beer is its Fat Tire

amber ale, but booming sales have helped fuel a bustling, eclectic lineup that includes Belgian-style ales to wheat beer, their Shift pale lager ("when your work is done, you'll want one"), and the intriguing Lips of Faith series, which makes room for brews that use all kinds of left-field ingredients such as coconut, peppers, and pluot juice. Save us a Salted Belgian Chocolate Stout.

**Connecticut:** Stratford's Two Roads Brewing Company set up shop in a century-old building and poured $18 million into turning it into a state-of-the-art beermaking facility. There's also Plainville's Relic Brewing Company, where brewmaster Mark Sigman promotes a "small, experimental" aesthetic. To whit: the brewery's Belgian IPA brewed with orange blossom honey, amarillo, and mosaic hops.

**Delaware:** If you've done any kind of craft beer drinking, you know about the magic that is Delaware's Dogfish Head, a favorite among discerning beerhounds since the mid-1990s

and a reliable source of unusual and high-ABV brews. Delaware's first brewpub, Dogfish Head has made a habit of pushing the beer envelope, bottling everything from its vaunted IPA line to more unusual stuff like Namaste (a Belgian-style beer brewed with orange slices, coriander, and lemongrass) and its Ancient Ales line, which lives up to its name by using centuries-old brewing techniques—and even ingredients—culled from archaeological digs.

**Florida:** Cigar City Brewing in Tampa has only been brewing since 2009, but already boasts an award-winning line of beers that includes a flagship Imperial Stout as well as a host of intriguing brews like Right Side Up Pineapple Cake Lager, Guava Grove Sour Ale, and Chicory Dickory Choc Brown Ale. Who needs Disney World?

*For part 2 of*
*"The United States of Beer,"*
*turn to page 161.*

# BILLY BEER

Billy Beer initially seemed poised for success. It was, after all, endorsed by Billy Carter, the former gas station owner who rose to national fame in the late '70s by virtue of being the affable, boozy redneck brother of President Jimmy Carter. Whether you loved, hated, or were indifferent to Carter's politics, the idea of guzzling a brew named after his family's black sheep had a certain delicious appeal, and every can came emblazoned with Billy's wryly funny promise: "I had this beer brewed just for me. It's the best beer I've ever tasted. And I've tasted a lot."

Unfortunately for Falls City Brewing, the Louisville brewer behind Billy Beer, few consumers shared that effusive opinion—not even Carter himself, who had a habit of telling reporters that he was still a Pabst Blue Ribbon man.

Less than a year after debuting the beer, Falls City was out of business, and although unopened cans have periodically enjoyed surges in value on the collector's market, Billy Beer's chief value over the last few decades has been as a definitive 1970s reference and punch line.

\* \* \*

## 9 REAL BAR NAMES

**1.** The 13th Step

**2.** Club Foot

**3.** Burp Castle

**4.** Ugly Toona Saloona

**5.** Bar Bar Black Sheep Chicago

**6.** High Dive

**7.** He's Not Here

**8.** Third Base ("the last stop before home")

**9.** Warm Beer and Lousy Food

# THE WISDOM OF BILLY CARTER

"There is no such thing as a bad beer. It's that some taste better than others."

"I'm a real Southern boy. I got a red neck, white socks, and Blue Ribbon beer."

"But that won't give me a free hand to hold the beer." (While learning a two-handed backhand during a tennis lesson.)

"Marijuana is like Coors beer. If you could buy the damn stuff at a Georgia filling station, you'd decide you wouldn't want it."

"Paintings are like a beer, only beer tastes good and it's hard to stop drinking beer."

"Beer is not a good cocktail-party drink, especially in a home where you don't know where the bathroom is."

# MAKE YOUR OWN BEER IN TWO HOURS

*Drinking beer is obviously a lot of fun, but brewing it can be a blast, too. The process can seem fairly daunting to anyone who's never done it, but it's really pretty painless and quick.*

## WHAT YOU NEED

Start off with a starter brewing kit. A good one will include everything (or nearly everything) you need to get started. At any rate, you'll need a fermenting bucket with a lid, or a glass fermenter with an airlock cap, a glass thermometer, a racking cane, tubing, a tubing clamp, and sanitizer. You'll also need a large stockpot (around five gallons), a funnel, a strainer, 12-ounce bottles, and mesh bags. Hopefully, your town has a brewing supply store; if not, you can always turn to sites like homebrew.org.

## GET CLEAN

Even if your gear is new, it still needs to be cleaned—thoroughly—because a little unwelcome bacteria can ruin your entire brew. Fill your fermenting bucket or stockpot with five gallons of water, throw in all your new brewing tools, and add a few ounces of brewing sanitizer (Star San is the most used brand), put the lid on, and shake it up until the sanitizer has been properly spread. Wash and sanitize your hands with the same stuff, and rinse and dry your equipment.

## THE YEAST OF YOUR WORRIES

In addition to equipment, you'll need the beer ingredients themselves, such as yeast. The grains and hops you'll use will vary, but yeast is more straightforward. We recommend you use liquid yeast packs (made by manufacturers such as Wyeast), which contain an activator pouch that's released into the mix after you thwack the pouch against a hard surface like the palm of your hand. Smack it, shake it up, and watch the pouch inflate—but don't break the bag.

## GET TO BREWING

Add two to three gallons of water to your clean, empty, and dry five-gallon pot and bring it to a boil. It's at this point that you take one of your mesh bags and pour in some flavoring grains, like roasted barley; the bag steeps in the water until it reaches 170°F, which generally takes about half an hour. If you hit 170 before 30 minutes have passed, remove the pot from the heat and let the grains steep until the full half-hour has elapsed.

After you've steeped your grains, remove the bag and turn off your heat. Here's where you'll want to add your malt extract (we'd recommend using the liquid variety to start), stirring it to make sure none of it sticks to the bottom of the pot. Now you've got wort, and it's time to boil it, watching carefully; when foam starts to rise, blow on it or turn down the heat until the foam drops to avoid boilovers, then bring it back up until you've got a good boil going.

Now it's time to start thinking about hops. Depending on what type of brew you're making and which extracts you're using, your process will vary. Essentially, that foaming stage you reached while boiling the wort is called a "hot break," and once you reach it, you're doing what's called boiling for additions—following the instructions for whatever hops are called for in your brew. If you're adding flavoring or aroma hops in addition to hopped extract, then your boiling process will take about half an hour; if you're using hopped extract and not adding extra hops, that drops to about 15 minutes. Either way, you're adding flavor to your beer here, so make sure you show those hops some love as you're adding them.

When your boil is in the home stretch (about five minutes left), it's time to add whatever finishing agents you're going to drop in to encourage proteins to drop out;

many brewers use Whirlfloc, a commercial blend that uses Irish moss and purified carrageenan.

Once your boil is finished, it's time to cool your wort. If you're using a five-gallon kettle, you can do this in the sink or bathtub by using cold tap water or an ice bath (this is called a "partial boil"); if you're using a larger kettle ("full boil"), you can use a wort chiller, which wraps metal coils around the kettle for an immersion cooling that you achieve by hooking the chiller up to a tap. Either way, the faster you get your wort down to what's called yeast pitching temperature (65–90°F), the better it is for your brew. Be careful to keep the lid on your kettle during this process to prevent any contaminants from working their way in.

While your kettle is cooling, dump the sanitizing solution out of your fermenting bucket. If you're using a five-gallon kettle, add two gallons of cold water and/or ice to the bucket, and remember—the cleaner, the better. Filtered water and store-bought ice will go a long way toward

preventing odd flavors from popping up in your brew later on, so go the extra mile by running your tap water through a carbon filter and refraining from using those old ice cubes tucked away in the back of your freezer.

Once your wort has cooled, it's time to transfer. This process will vary depending on whether you've gone the full-boil or partial-boil route, but either way, here's where you'll pitch your yeast into the fermenting vessel, then add your wort. That adding process can be as simple as pouring the contents of your kettle into the bucket (this is the only stage of the brewing process where exposing your brew, however briefly, to the open air is a good thing), or as fancy as using a full-boil kettle that transfers its contents to the fermenting vessel with a spigot.

Once you've done all that, put your vessel in a spot where it'll stay undisturbed (and at around 65–70°F) for the next 14 days.

It definitely bears mentioning that this doesn't take into account the rest of the process—like, say, bottling, which requires its own set of instructions—and we've really just skimmed the surface of brewing, which involves a lot of variables and can be as complicated as you want it to be. What we hope we've made clear here, though, is that brewing can be pretty quick and easy; if you've got a little extra money for equipment and ingredients, and a couple of hours for running through these basic steps, your own beer is closer than you might think.

# MORE STRANGE BEER FLAVORS

**Oysters.** Have you ever wondered what the rich, coffee-and-chocolate flavor profile of a stout would taste like with just the faintest hint of seafood? Of course you haven't. But the Oysterhead Stout from Magnolia Brewing, brewed with dozens of pounds of oyster shells, is worth a try.

**Sriracha.** Sriracha is that suddenly omnipresent condiment made from chili peppers, vinegar, and garlic. It's pretty hot stuff, which makes for the challenging Sriracha from Rogue Brewery.

**Ghost peppers.** Even hotter is Palmetto Brewing's Ghost Rider. It's an American pale ale, but hardly pedestrian…or refreshing. It's spiced with smoked ghost peppers, among the spiciest peppers on earth. Palmetto recommends pairing it with smoked meats, and, understandably, a glass of milk.

# VERY OLD DRINKING GAMES

**The Puzzle Jug.** Modern drinking games tend to be a vulgar macho display more than a true test of skill. In the 14th century, drinkers devised something far more devilish: the Puzzle Jug, a hilarious test of mental acuity that was both shamelessly wasteful and definitely fun. Here's how it worked: A jug was designed with a series of holes that needed to be covered in a certain way in order to prevent the drinker from spilling the contents all over his shirt…a task that obviously grew more difficult as more beers were consumed. To add insult to injury, the jugs also tended to be inscribed with challenges, which the chagrined party had plenty of time to read while wringing out his shirt and mopping up the floor.

**Kottabos.** Centuries before college students invented Beer Pong, the ancient Greeks tested their inebriated aim during rounds of kottabos, a game

that involved hucking the yeast deposits at the bottoms of their glasses at a target in the middle of the room. It wasn't quite as raucous as it sounds; kottabos was a fairly regimented game, requiring players to remain in the Greek drinker's customary reclined position and use only his right arm to send the glass flying without splitting apart.

**Nagelspielen.** Combining a number of seemingly disparate ingredients—alcohol, axes, and nails—Nagelspielen (roughly "playing with nails" in German) dates back at least as far as the original Oktoberfest in 1810. The rules are simple: Each player tries to drive a nail into a stump, one swing of the axe at a time, with the winner claiming a free drink. It isn't quite as easy as it might sound; for starters, players have to use the sharp end of the axe, and the presence of rowdy bar patrons jeering you as the nail inevitably bends, requiring the expenditure of precious turns to try to straighten it out, adds up to all kinds of fun frustration. These days, the game is generally played as Hammerschlagen—which has contestants play

with the wedge end of a three-pound blacksmith's hammer rather than an axe—but the end result remains the same: drunk people swinging heavy objects in a crowded room.

**Buffalo Club.** Many drinking games rely on props of some sort, but to be a member of the Buffalo Club, all you need are two hands and some booze. The general idea, which allegedly dates back to the Wild West custom of keeping one's dominant hand free during recreational activities so as to be ready for a quick-draw shootout at any time, is that players must always drink with their nondominant hand. If another Buffalo Club member spots you breaking the rule, he or she yells "Buffalo!" to signal that you have to pound your drink as quickly as possible (not as easy as it might seem when you're surrounded by a room full of people screaming "Buffalo!" in your face). If you call "Buffalo!" and you're wrong about the other player's dominant hand, however, you have to pound your own drink.

Buffalo Club's main twist is that it's a life-time game, and one that members tend to take fairly seriously; in the U.S., you can even join the American Buffalo Club Association, which has chapters in most states.

**Beer Runs.** In an effort to purge the previous weekend's hangover with a little hair of the dog, British colonists in what is now Malaysia would gather on Monday evenings for a "paper chase." A runner designated the "hare" would lead the pack by laying down a trail of paper bits or chalk marks, and at the finish line, everyone would celebrate with a few rounds. There's also the Kastenlauf, a German walking race of three to seven miles whose participants, united in teams of two, work to carry and consume a crate of beer before crossing the finish line. An American variant of this is The Beer Mile, in which participants run laps equating a mile, pausing after a lap to drink a can or pint of beer.

# BEERS NAMED AFTER GREAT WRITERS AND ARTISTS

**Shakespeare Stout.** An oatmeal stout by any other name would taste as sweet, as Juliet from *Romeo and Juliet* might say. But regardless of whether the Bard's writing really has anything to do with Shakespeare Stout from Oregon's Rogue Ales, it's still a tasty (and award-winning) tribute.

**Walt Wit.** The Walt Whitman Bridge runs between Philadelphia and Gloucester City in New Jersey and traverses the Delaware River. That was where Whitman once sat and watched the "approaching sunset of unusual splendor, a broad tumble of clouds, with much golden haze and profusion of beaming shaft and dazzle" that he later described in "Only a New Ferry Boat." Thus inspired, the Philadelphia Brewing Company developed Walt Wit, a cleverly named Belgian witbier whose recipe boasts a tumble of natural

flavors appropriate for the poet who wrote *Leaves of Grass*. (Walt Wit contains no leaves or grass.)

**Oscar Wilde.** Given the rather awful circumstances of his later life and death (imprisoned for homosexuality and worked to death at a labor camp), one might expect an Oscar Wilde beer to be loaded up with the bitterest of hops. The UK's Mighty Oak Brewing Company took the opposite approach, opting for a recipe with the sparkling lightness of the legendarily insouciant wit that led the younger Wilde to come up with quotes like the one emblazoned on the beer that bears his name: "Work is the curse of the drinking class."

**Longfellow Winter Ale.** If Maine had an official brewery, it'd probably be Shipyard, and if the state had an official poet, he'd probably be Henry Wadsworth Longfellow—and since both of them were born in Portland, it's only fitting that Shipyard should honor the 19th-century superstar of verse with its Longfellow Winter Ale. In his 1855 poem "My Lost Youth," Longfellow recalled

the "black wharves and the ships, and the sea tides tossing free" of his youth. Shipyard's brew does what it can to bottle those memories with a dark, bittersweet beer, good for downing on rocky shorelines while looking out at lighthouses on stormy coasts.

**Thomas Hardy's Ale.** Originally brewed by Eldridge Pope Brewery in 1968 to commemorate the 40th anniversary of Thomas Hardy's death, Thomas Hardy's Ale was inspired by a passage from his 1880 novel *The Trumpet Major*, describing a beer that had "the most beautiful colour an artist could possibly desire, as bright as an autumn sunset." Produced once a year in limited quantities, Thomas Hardy's Ale became an annual event for beer connoisseurs, many of whom were devastated when the company closed its doors in 2003. Like Hardy's works, however, the beer that bears his name lives on; it was resurrected by O'Hanlons Brewery, which stopped bottling it in 2008, and then again in 2013, when a company called Brew Invest announced plans to bring it back a second time.

**Pliny the Elder.** One of the forefathers of botany, Pliny the Elder lived in Italy during the first century AD. Among his many accomplishments before being killed by a volcano: He's alleged to have discovered hops—and although that's impossible to verify, it was enough for the Russian River Brewing Company to name their double IPA after him. Believed by many experts to be the best beer bottled in the U.S., Pliny the Elder is highly sought after, especially in markets outside Russian River's West Coast distribution range.

**Grünewald Porter and Goya Stout.** Nobody knows how to get messed up like an artist, right? That may have been the thinking at Santa Fe's Duel Brewing when they named beers after painters Matthias Grünewald and Francisco Goya. Both beers boast an ABV north of 11 percent—which may have you seeing (or hearing or tasting) colors.

# MORE OF THE WORLD'S MOST EXPENSIVE BEERS

*Another round of the bottle shock
that began on page 90.*

**Beer:** Antarctic Nail Nale
**Price:** $800
**Story:** Brewed using water melted from a chunk of Antarctic iceberg, this 10% ABV pale ale is mostly a gimmick, and an expensive one at that; the abbreviated 30-bottle run made its debut at an auction, where the first bottle went for $800. But unlike brewers who've prowled to the ends of the earth to dig up rare ingredients mostly for shock value, the folks at Nail Brewing did it all for a good cause: 100% of the profits from Antarctic Nail Ale were donated to the Sea Shepherd Conservation Society.

**Beer:** Schorschbock 57
**Price:** $275
**Story:** Not only one of the world's most expensive beers, this Schorschbräu brew also claims to be the

strongest: 57.5% ABV. Produced in a tiny 36-bottle run in 2011, Schorschbock 57 is also pretty darn rare—although judging from the mostly quite scornful reviews posted at RateBeer ("the taste is dark tangy fruit, cinnamon, syrupy, toffee, brown bread, salted beef, nail polish remover and gasoline"), that probably isn't such a bad thing.

**Beer:** PBR 1844
**Price:** $44
**Story:** If you were to ask any random drinker to name the three letters least likely to be found sitting next to one another on a list of the world's most expensive beer, the most common answer would probably be "P, B, and R." But PBR 1844 is no joke. Here in the States, the blue ribbon affixed to cans of Pabst is rarely taken seriously; in China, however, PBR is truly a premium brew—it's made using a list of fancy ingredients that includes German caramel malts, aged in uncharred American whiskey barrels. It's even served in beautiful, fancy bottles. Sadly, it's off-limits to U.S. drinkers…at least for now.

**Beer:** Samuel Adams Utopia
**Price:** $150
**Story:** Quite a few of the beers on this list are only available to American drinkers as imports, but Sam Adams' Utopias are a homegrown premium brew; in fact, at $150 for each fancy 700-ml bottle, it's the most expensive beer made in the U.S. Getting it can be kind of tricky, depending on where you live, because its 27% ABV runs afoul of certain states' beer laws, and it's only produced every two years.

But if you're able to get your hands around a bottle, it's an experience worth pursuing for the beer enthusiast. Each batch is aged up to 18 years in an assortment of casks, boasts a list of ingredients that includes maple syrup, and has provoked a rather rapturous buzz among the faithful, who point to its distinctive mouthfeel and blend of flavors as making it one of the few premium beers that actually lives up to its name.

**Beer:** Sink the Bismarck

**Price:** $80 for a six-pack

**Story:** Another premium drinking experience from BrewDog, this insane "quadruple IPA" weighs in at a punishing 41% ABV, what the company rather understatedly refers to as "beer, amplified" and suggests that drinkers give "the same amount of skeptical, tentative respect you would show an international chess superstar, clown, or gypsy." At $80 for a sixer, you'd better at least pay attention to this stuff while you're guzzling away.

**Beer:** Unnamed

**Price:** $2,650

**Story:** For a 2014 episode of their reality show *Brew Dogs*, beer-makers James Watt and Martin Dickie set out to make the most expensive beer possible…because they were in Las Vegas. Ingredients included dark chocolate, saffron, black truffles, and gold flakes. The bottle was auctioned off to benefit Keep Memory Alive, an Alzheimer's foundation.

# YOUR DAD'S BEER, PART 1

*You don't have to seek out obscure regional labels or make your own to enjoy a fine brew; after all, our dads got along just fine with these old standbys.*

**Pabst:** In 1844, Jacob Best founded the Empire Brewery in Milwaukee, which later became Best and Company. When Best's son Philip took over in 1860, he changed it to the Philip Best Brewing Co. Best's daughter then married a ship captain named Frederick Pabst, who purchased a chunk of the business, and by 1880 he was president of the largest brewery in America.

Pabst's glory days lasted a good long while and fed handsomely into the Milwaukee econ-omy—not just because the brewery hosted lavish tours that culminated in endless free refills at the in-house pub, but also because Pabst plowed its largesse back into the city by purchasing a tract of

land along Whitefish Bay and building a popular destination resort.

Of course, we wouldn't be talking about any of this if it weren't for the beer: Pabst Blue Ribbon, which started out as Best Select in 1875. At festivals, Pabst took to draping a silk ribbon around the bottles, leading some drinkers to call it the company's "blue ribbon" beer even though it hadn't *actually* won one. Frederick Pabst, a crafty businessman, renamed the beer.

PBR remained one of the best-selling beers in the world until the 1980s, when it started to seem stodgy next to the sleeker and better-advertised beers being pumped out by Budweiser, Coors, and Miller. The company found itself vulnerable to hostile takeover during the age of corporate raid-ers, and that's what happened in 1985, when S&P Co. purchased Pabst. Production was contracted out, the historic Pabst brewery was shut down, and operations were moved first to San Antonio, and then to Los Angeles.

While the iconic, nostalgic PBR label is exactly the kind of thing a certain type of drinker will look for during a bout of semi-ironic drinking, the Pabst Brewing Company itself has become a sort of holding company for previously defunct labels. Ballantine, Lone Star, Rainier, Schlitz, and Stroh are just a few of the brands that have been taken over by Pabst.

**Rolling Rock:** It's the flagship beer of the Latrobe Brewing Company, which got its start in 1893. Local legend has it that the same order of Benedictine monks who originally settled the region were also Latrobe's first brewmasters and helped get the company off to a roaring start.

When the U.S. went dry, so did Latrobe, but the company rebounded after Prohibition ended. Anticipating a bright future for beer, the Tito brothers (Frank, Robert, Ralph, and Anthony) purchased the company while Prohibition was still in effect, and their gamble paid off handsomely. Between 1933 and 1939, the Titos brewed a

couple of popular varieties, Latrobe Old German and Latrobe Pilsner. But things really took off in 1939 when they introduced Rolling Rock, an extra-pale lager whose distinctive bottle promised to bring quality Latrobe product "from the mountain streams to you."

Recognizing that Depression-era customers would need to stretch their drinking dollar, Latrobe offered Rolling Rock in two sizes: a cheap, 7-ounce bottle (referred to as a "pony") and a 12-ounce (a "horse"). The beer became a local favorite, and unlike a lot of other American businessmen, the Titos were perfectly content to enjoy their status as regional kings of beer.

Affordability helped fuel Rolling Rock's rise, as did its uncomplicated, dependable taste. But its success was also owed largely to what might accurately be described as its mystique—notably the mysterious "33" emblazoned on the back of every bottle. There are plenty of theories as to why it's there, but no one really knows, not even the folks

at the brewery…or if they do, they've never spilled the beans.

After a long, mid-century sales slump, the Titos sold Latrobe Brewing Company in 1985 to a buyout firm whose managers intended to pump up the company's marketing in the short term in order to resell it for a profit. Labatt took over in 1987 and spent the next 15 years ramping up the beer's market share while building a "lifestyle brand" that eventually included a hugely popular local outdoor festival.

The good times were not to last. In 1995, Labatt was purchased by Belgium's Interbrew, which became InBev and sold Rolling Rock to Anheuser-Busch, leaving the Latrobe Brewing Company facility without a beer to produce, and Latrobe itself without hundreds of jobs.

Rolling Rock ended up being brewed in New Jersey, a huge blow to the Latrobe economy. The Latrobe facility was ultimately sold off to City

Brewing, and became a contract facility to produce beers such as Guinness Blonde and Sam Adams Oktoberfest.

**Molson:** Yuengling, founded in 1829, is the oldest brewer in the U.S., but not in North America. That honor goes to Molson, which got its start in 1786 when British immigrant John Molson purchased a small Montreal brewhouse and used it as the starting point for an empire.

Part of Molson's success stemmed from his ability to brew beer people liked, but he was also a savvy businessman. He only started a brewery in the first place because he saw a market for intoxicating beverages cheaper than wine or rum, and he opted to cater to the waves of beer-loving English and Irish drinkers emigrating to Canada.

In the 1940s, the company went public, using the cash to fuel a series of ventures that included purchasing the Montreal Canadiens hockey team (perhaps not coincidentally, today Molson is the

official beer of the NHL). By the early 1990s, they'd purchased the Carling O'Keefe brewing conglomerate, making Molson the largest brewing company in Canada.

Of course, not even the largest brewing company in Canada is immune to the increasingly global nature of corporate beer, and in 2005, Molson merged with Coors, consolidating both parties' considerable assets to form what at the time ranked as the seventh-largest corporation in the beer business.

**Labatt:** In 1847, Ontario brewers Samuel Eccles and John Kinder Labatt partnered to form Labatt and Eccles. Eccles retired shortly thereafter, selling his interest to Labatt, who renamed the company the London Brewery. After Labatt's death in 1866, his son took over and steered the newly named Labatt Brewing Company.

So strong were Labatt's finances that the company managed to weather the double whammy

of Canadian Prohibition (1916) and its American cousin (1919), a long dry scourge that wiped out all but 15 of eastern Canada's breweries by the time it was finally over. With the brewing herd thinned, Labatt was in position to strengthen its hold on the marketplace. By the 1950s, it was a publicly traded behemoth whose light ale, Labatt 50, was the nation's best-selling beer from 1950 until 1979…when it was succeeded by Labatt Blue.

Various corporate mergers have since made Labatt a subsidiary of InBev. And although it remains a market leader in Canada, Molson has suffered a steep decline in the U.S., where its sales plummeted nearly 30 percent in the last decade.

*For the stories behind more classic brews, turn to page 211.*

# BEER IS GOOD FOR YOU!

• Beer contains trace amounts of silicon, and according to a 2008 study published in *Food and Chemical Toxicology*, that silicon may reduce the body's ability to absorb aluminum. Less aluminum in the bloodstream and brain means a reduced risk for Alzheimer's disease.

• Barley, from which beer is most often made, is loaded with ferulic acid, an antioxidant that protects the skin against sun damage. A 2000 study in England found that the ferulic acid in beer is more absorbable and useful to the body than when it's found in other crops, such as tomatoes and corn.

• A 2010 study of 38,000 men found that when nondrinkers took up a glass-a-day beer habit, their risk of developing type 2 diabetes decreased by 25 percent.

• In a study at Tufts University in 2009, test subjects responded well to the calcium content in beer. Participants enjoyed a higher level of bone density.

• Beer may be the most effective preventive medicine against kidney stones. A Finnish study concluded that regular beer drinking may reduce the development of the painful blockages by 40 percent. Why? Beer is high in water, but compounds in hops slow the seepage of calcium from bone, which is how the stones first form.

• A 2013 study at Greece's Harokopio University determined that moderate beer consumption boosted arterial flexibility—that means it protects against hardening arteries.

• Numerous studies indicate that beer raises good cholesterol and lowers bad cholesterol…in moderate consumption. More than one or two servings a day can weaken heart muscles.

# BEER MOVIES

***Beerfest* (2006)** After making the cult comedy *Super Troopers* and horror satire *Club Dread*, the Broken Lizard comedy troupe made this movie, about a pair of brothers out to reclaim their family's honor by competing in a secret beer-drinking Olympics operated by their evil German cousins.

***Strange Brew* (1983)** If beer cinema has a *Citizen Kane*, it's *Strange Brew,* the big-screen *SCTV* spinoff starring Rick Moranis and Dave Thomas as the dim-witted, beer-swilling Canadians Bob and Doug McKenzie. It tracks the McKenzies' attempt to get free beer by planting a live mouse

in a bottle and complaining to the brewer, only to stumble onto the brewery owner's evil plan. Janet Maslin wrote in her review for the *New York Times*, "Anyone who's partial to the McKenzies' humor doubtless has a fondness for beer."

OPEN BEER HERE

***Beer* (1985)** Beer commercials are often so ridiculous that they border on self-parody. Their often desperate attempts to sell a lifestyle instead of a beverage inspired this satire about an advertising agency that builds a beer ad campaign around three beer-drinking doofuses who foil a bar robbery.

***Beer Wars* (2001)** One of the few movies on this list that isn't a sophomoric comedy, this 2001 documentary by filmmaker Anat Baron details the craft brew industry's struggle to carve out and maintain market share amid the major conglomerates. Things have changed a great deal in the years since *Beer Wars* was released—in favor of the small-batch breweries—but the film provides great historical context.

***What! No Beer?* (1933)** This comedy stars Buster Keaton and Jimmy Durante as a

pair of buds who try to take over a defunct brewery in anticipation of Prohibition being repealed, only to run afoul of a local mobster.

**American Beer (2004)** Part beer documentary, part real-life road comedy, this 2004 release chronicles the adventures of four friends on a cross-country drive to California, punctuated by their visits to microbreweries along the way (a list that includes such noteworthy establishments as Dogfish Head, Shipyard, Victory, Sierra Nevada, Anchor, New Belgium Brewing Company, and many more). While the film wasn't exactly a box-office sensation, it did lead to one crucial drinking development: Barcade, a chain of hybrid bar/arcades co-founded by *American Beer* director Paul Kermizian.

**The Saddest Music in the World (2003)** It looks like it was filmed in the 1930s, but that isn't even the weirdest thing about this surreal dramedy about a brewery owner (Isabella Rossellini) seeking to drum up publicity for her company during

Prohibition's waning days. She sponsors a contest offering $25,000 to the person who can create the saddest music in the world. A highlight: transparent prosthetic legs full of beer.

**Smokey and the Bandit (1977)** It's not just a road movie, or a mustache movie (see Burt Reynolds's luxurious lip hair); *Smokey* is definitely a beer film. The plot hinges on a legendary driver (Reynolds) hired by a bootlegger to ferry 400 cases of Coors across state lines. It's hard to fathom now, but in 1977, that was highly illegal. The movie's $128 million gross makes it the top-earning beer movie of all time; it was the third-biggest draw of 1977, trailing only *Star Wars* and *Close Encounters of the Third Kind*.

# THE HOWS AND WHYS OF NONALCOHOLIC BEER

Let's be honest: Beer is an acquired taste. Even the world's most enthusiastic tipplers may not have enjoyed their first few pints, and really getting into the complexities and varieties of the stuff can take quite a while; it's part of the reason why sweet malt beverages and hard cider have always had their place in the market. Like a timid person entering a swimming pool on a cool day, some people's taste buds need time to acclimate to beer. The fact that it contains alcohol likely speeds up the process.

But for the subset of drinkers who really enjoy beer but can't ingest alcohol for whatever reason, there are nonalcoholic, or NA, brews. They've always endured a bad rap, and even the most popular brands (O'Doul's, Sharp's, etc.) tend to collect dust on rarely visited store shelves.

For a lot of people, the thought of drinking it is comical. Beer without alcohol? Why would a person even bother? Lots of reasons, with a lot of history behind them. Up through the 19th century in England, the water was far too polluted to drink, so the populace—children included—drank beer, because brewing processed out most of the toxins. But even in the miserable world of 1700s England, people didn't want or need to get drunk in the morning (or they were children), so they drank something called "small ale"—beer with an alcohol content of 2 to 3 percent. This beer wasn't that different from the ales sold (albeit in small quantities) in the United States during Prohibition. Yes, you could buy beer under Prohibition—commercial brewers stayed in business by bottling beer that stayed below the 0.5% ABV legal limit.

If making great regular beer is a science, then brewing one that is both tasty and free (or almost free) of alcohol is even trickier. And as anyone who's ever sipped a mass-market NA beer can tell

you, that's most definitely the case. Once people stop making fun of the idea of NA beer long enough to actually try it, they tend to start in all over again on the flavor, which can run the gamut from bland to outright rank. There are a number of good reasons for this, most of which can be traced back to the fact that, in order to brew non-alcoholic beer, you start out like you're making the regular stuff, but before anyone can drink it, you have to take the alcohol out. Sounds difficult, right? It is.

Traditionally, the most cost-effective method involves heating the brew. Alcohol's boiling point is well below water's, so if you put it under just enough heat—roughly 173°F—you'll eventually end up with nonalcoholic beer. The problem, though, is that it's just cooked the other ingredients, which results in a concoction that doesn't taste right. Brewers can combat this with vacuum

distilling, which lowers the boiling point considerably and helps ward off some of those flavor problems, but it isn't a perfect solution.

Over the years, brewers have devised a number of other methods. One of the most effective is reverse osmosis, a process that sends the beer through a filter that only allows water and alcohol through, distills the water-alcohol mixture and removes the alcohol, and then sends the leftover liquid back into the brewing grains. It isn't as

cheap or easy as simply boiling out the alcohol, but it results in an end product that tastes more like real beer.

We can debate the merits of beer without alcohol, but absolutely no one enjoys a flat beer—which is unfortunately what you're left with after you've boiled or filtered out alcohol. That's because the carbonation

in beer is a by-product of yeast turning sugar into alcohol. In short, no alcohol = no bubbles.

The most popular solution to this problem is to inject $CO_2$ back in, but that adds its own set of headaches, chief among them an unpleasant flavor with sour, metallic overtones.

Basically, beer's flavor is a delicate thing, the result of countless complicated factors and compounds that can't help but be altered when a brewer mucks around with its basic components. Hope may be on the horizon, however. Modern science, always working hard to make us happy, has uncovered a way of extracting aromatic gas compounds from regular beer, condensing them, and injecting them into NA beer, thus more closely approximating that old-fashioned flavor.

# THE MOST POPULAR BEERS ON EARTH

**United States:** Bud Light

**Canada:** Budweiser

**Mexico:** Corona

**Argentina:** Cerveza Quilmes

**Brazil:** Skol

**Venezuela:** Cerveza Polar

**Jamaica:** Red Stripe

**England:** Carling

**Germany:** Krombacher

**Poland:** Zywiec

**Romania:** Ursus

**Russia:** Baltika

**Italy:** Peroni

**Czech Republic:** Pilsner Urquell

**Belgium:** Chimay

**Ireland:** Guinness

**Scotland:** Tennent's Lager

**The Netherlands:** Heineken

**Denmark:** Carlsberg

**Norway:** Ringnes

**Iceland:** Víking Gylltur

**Finland:** Karhu

**India:** Kingfisher

**Pakistan:** Murree

**Israel:** Goldstar

**Turkey:** Efes

**China:** Snow

**Cambodia:** Angkor

**Laos:** Beerlao

**Singapore:** Tiger

**Thailand:** Singha

**Kenya:** Tusker

**Indonesia:** Bintang

**Japan:** Asahi Super Dry

**South Korea:** Hite

**Philippines:** San Miguel Pale Pilsen

**Ethiopia:** St. George

**South Africa:** Castle Lager

**Australia:** Victoria Bitter

# A BEER FOR EVERYTHING

**Beer for dogs!** Sharing a six-pack with your dog is a pretty horrible idea, not least because hops are toxic to them. So what's a dog lover to do when seized by the urge to pop the cap off a bottle of beer and pour it into his or her favorite furry friend's dish? Enter Bowser Beer, a rather disgusting-sounding concoction that blends meat broth and malt barley into a nonalcoholic, non-carbonated, beef- or chicken-flavored beverage that your dog will be able to pound without getting sick. At $20 for a sixer, it's probably not the kind of thing you'd want to buy every day.

**Beer for kids!** You probably know that Europeans tend to be far more relaxed about drinking than Americans. But in Belgium, beer has a long tradition as

a family drink, specifically *tafelbier* ("table beer"), a brew made with such a low alcohol percentage (anywhere between 1 and 3 percent) that it's generally thought of as a cousin to root beer. Tafelbier has fallen out of favor somewhat with younger generations and has been largely replaced by soda, contributing to an increase in juvenile obesity that alarmed some Belgians enough to propose serving tafelbier in schools. The proposal was actually tested in one school in 2001. Unsurprisingly, many kids said they preferred tafelbier to soda, but parents still couldn't abide serving beer at school to kids, and it didn't catch on.

**Beer for breakfast!** For most of us, "beer for breakfast" is the exclusive domain of trembling alcoholics, but there's actually a small-but-serious school of thought that argues there's absolutely nothing wrong with cracking a cold one to start the day. To that end, some brewers have marketed breakfast-friendly beers with slightly tongue-in-cheek names. For example, there's, uh, Breakfast, the since-retired cherry wheat cereal-like lager

once sold by New Zealand's Moa Brewing Company. In the U.S., morning drinkers can look for beers such as the Santa Fe Brewing Company's Imperial Java Stout, whose can comes helpfully emblazoned with the image of a coffee cup and the legends "before noon," and "not for use with donuts," or Founders Brewing Company's descriptively named Breakfast Stout.

**More beer for breakfast!** For the somewhat more traditionally inclined, there's Colorado's Black Bottle Brewery, where owner Sean Nook made headlines in 2014 by buying up every box of Count Chocula cereal in the Fort Collins area and using it as part of the recipe for a brew he dubbed Chocula Stout. Previous Black Bottle cereal-themed brews included beers that incorporated Golden Grahams, Cinnamon Toast Crunch, and Honey Bunches of Oats.

# THE UNITED STATES OF BEER, PART 2

**Georgia:** Commercial craft brewing in Georgia dates back to 1993, when the Atlanta Brewing Company (now Red Brick Brewing) got its start. There's also the Terrapin Beer Company, founded in 2002 by a pair of Atlanta Brewing defectors. After setting up shop in Athens, Terrapin enjoyed immediate success, taking home the American Pale Ale Gold Medal at the Great American Beer Festival in 2002. Other standouts include their 7.3% ABV Hopsecutioner IPA, and, of course, the Peach Farmhouse Ale.

**Hawaii:** You're probably more apt to imagine colorful cocktails with little umbrellas in them. But there's beer in paradise, too. Hawaii's most exported beer is Kona's Longboard Island Lager, which is fine, but doesn't offer the unique flavor characteristics you can find if you're lucky enough to sample some of Kona's less widely known beers,

like its Rift Zone Ale, brewed using yeast found in the rifts at Volcanoes National Park. That same spirit is embodied by the Maui Brewing Company, which brews Liquid Breadfruit, made with the titular ingredient and papaya seeds.

**Idaho:** Idaho's Grand Teton Brewing Company didn't start out with that name…or even in Idaho. Founded in 1988 as Otto Brothers, the company spent a decade in Wyoming before making the move; today, they sell more beer than any other brewer in the state, led by their hugely successful Ale 208, which boasts "100-percent Idaho-grown grain, hops, and pure Idaho spring water." In some parts of the state, they're outsold only by Bud and Bud Light.

**Illinois:** If it looks like a craft beer but is owned by a multinational megaconglomerate, is it still a craft beer? In the case of Chicago's Goose Island, purchased by Anheuser-Busch in 2011, the answer is yes. The new corporate overlords didn't change a thing; if anything, the deal freed up Goose Island

to expand its offerings, which include Matilda, a Belgian-style pale ale, as well as a reintroduced Nut Brown Ale, which had to be phased out before the sale because Goose Island didn't have enough facilities to produce it.

**Indiana:** The apparent favorite in the John Cougar Mellencamp State is Munster's Three Floyds Brewing Company. Founded in 1996 by brothers Nick and Simon Floyd, along with their dad, Mike Floyd, the company boasts not only the highest rated beers in Indiana, but some of the most beloved (and well-named) small brews anywhere. A partial list: Dark Lord Russian Imperial Stout, Dreadnought Imperial IPA, Behemoth Barleywine, Baller Stout, Permanent Funeral Double IPA, and Zombie Dust American Pale Ale.

**Iowa:** The Hawkeye State's preeminent brewer is undoubtedly Toppling Goliath, whose towering stature on the relatively young Iowa craft brew scene befits its name. Purveyor of signature brews like the Assassin, Kentucky Brunch, and

Mornin' Delight Imperial Stout, as well as lighter offerings such as the Light Speed Pale Ale and a wide variety of single and double IPAs, Toppling Goliath is a favorite among Midwestern beer connoisseurs. They've got emerging competition from local favorites like Backpocket Brewing (try the Slingshot Dunkel) and Peace Tree Brewing, known for their Hop Sutra Double IPA.

**Kansas:** The Free State Brewing Company's offerings are led by their well-loved Owd Macs Imperial Stout, Old Backus Barleywine, and Cloud Hopper Imperial IPA. But they've got company, including the Tallgrass Brewing Company, whose burgeoning lineup includes a sought-after porter dubbed the Zombie Monkie, the Ethos IPA and Oasis Ale, and a sweet stout named Vanilla Bean Buffalo Sweat.

**Kentucky:** The Bluegrass State is known far more for its bourbon than its beer, and in fact, you can come by quite a few bourbon-barrel-aged brews in Kentucky. That isn't all the local craft beer scene has to offer, however—just take a look

at what's pouring out of Louisville's Against the Grain Brewery. Co-founded by brewer Sam Cruz, whose love affair with beer goes back to his teen-age efforts to get around the legal drinking age by brewing his own at home, Against the Grain is home to a vast array of highly rated beers that includes its 70K Imperial Stout and Brett the Hipman Hop American Wild Ale.

**Louisiana:** The state offers a plethora of delicious and distinctive choices, including beers from the Parish Brewing Company (try their Farmhouse IPA), Bayou Teche (their Miel Savage is a vanilla-soaked delight), and NOLA (New Orleans Lager and Ale). But the cream of the crop might be the Abita Brewing Company, which not only offers some of the best beer in the state (including their Bourbon Street Barrel Aged Imperial Stout), but are admirably civic-minded, plunging a portion of the proceeds from their S.O.S. Weizen Pils back into restoration of the ravaged Gulf Coast.

*For part 3, turn to page 201.*

# BEERS NAMED AFTER MUSICIANS

**Bitches Brew.** Part imperial stout, part African mead, Dogfish Head's limited-edition brew sounds potentially punishing at 9% ABV, but it's a lot more complex than you might suspect. Miles Davis' Bitches Brew is kind of like Miles Davis's *Bitches Brew*, the classic album the jazz trumpeter released in 1970. Brewed in 2010 to commemorate the album's 40th anniversary, it's a solid choice for those who'd like to try something different and contemplate the experience while they're doing it…kind of like the album.

**Porkpie Hat Brew.** Given that jazz legend Lester Young was crippled by profound alcoholism that put him in the grave at age 50, naming a beer after him may seem insensitive. For fans of dark German lager, however, Angel City's Lester Young Porkpie Hat beer proved stellar—although, like Young himself, this brew is no longer with us.

**Wilco.** If you take the folks at Lagunitas at their word, this "rich, smooth, dangerous, and chocolatey" beer wasn't actually named after Wilco, Jeff Tweedy's beloved indie rock band. According to the brewery, they were just looking for a way to justify giving their 2010 springtime "recovery ale" a name that boiled down to the acronym WTF. Their original choice, Whiskey Tango Foxtrot, wasn't allowed because brewers can't legally put the word "whiskey" on a beer label. It's also got an extra Wilco connection in that "Foxtrot" references the band's seminal 2002 album, *Yankee Hotel Foxtrot*.

**Sleighr.** Ninkasi's holiday ale might be fudging a bit, because the name happens to be a twist on the name of metal gods Slayer. But on the other hand, it's a brew that comes with an umlaut—Ninkasi refers to it as a "dark doüble alt ale"—and what's more metal than an umlaut?

**Brother Ale Thelonious.** Like Thelonious Monk's jazz, North Coast Brewing Company's selection is robust and not for the amateur. In fact, at 9.3% ABV, you may want to take a nap after you finish the bottle. It's also civic-minded, as North Coast donates a portion of the profits from every sale to the Thelonious Monk Institute of Jazz, an organization dedicated to jazz education.

**Ozzy.** Naming your beer after a celebrity can help raise a brew's profile in a crowded marketplace and merit a mention in a silly beer trivia book, but the thing about famous people is that they tend to get a little cranky when you try to cash in on their celebrity without asking. The folks from Brewer's Art found themselves under legal assault from Ozzy Osbourne after bottling a Belgian-style ale they dubbed Ozzy, packaged with a logo depicting Osbourne's signature "OZZY" hand tattoo. Without much of a legal leg to stand on, the company made a name switch, redubbing the offending brew Beazly. Not very metal, but neither is getting sued.

Beer-Topia

# ZOMBIE BEER

*Some old-time beer brands are still around in
name only. They're not really the same beer,
brewed under contract, somewhere other than
their original brewery or city of origin.*

**Schlitz.** It's "the beer that made Milwaukee
famous," but it isn't the same beer that was first
brewed in 1849. The Schlitz company also owned
Stroh, both of which were sold off to Pabst in
1999.

**Ballantine.** In 1878, the Ballantine Brewing
Company of Newark, New Jersey, began producing
Ballantine IPA, one of the first India pale ales
available in the U.S. Initially quite popular in
the northeast, sales slowly dwindled until it disappeared by the 1970s. Pabst bought the rights
to Ballantine IPA in 1975…and resurrected it
in 2014.

*Beer-Topia*

**Lone Star.** The first major brewery in Texas was the Lone Star Brewery, built in San Antonio in 1884. That building is now the San Antonio Museum of Art. Lone Star Beer ("The National Beer of Texas") is produced by new owner Miller from a plant in Fort Worth, Texas.

**Henry Weinhard.** After 135 years as a low-cost favorite in the Pacific Northwest, its Portland brewery closed down in 1999. SABMiller bought the name, and the beer continues to be brewed at Full Sail Brewing in Hood River, Oregon.

**Blatz.** The Milwaukee brewery closed in 1959 after 109 years. It's still made, by Pabst, under contract by the brand's rights holder, Miller.

**Rainier.** This light lager is still available, and the Rainier Brewery still stands in Seattle…but Rainier beer isn't made there. In 1999, the company was sold to Stroh, then to Pabst, and Miller makes it today. The Rainier Brewery is now a processing center for Tully's Coffee.

# MAKE IT A LITE

About 50 years ago, 30 percent of American beer drinkers—overwhelmingly blue-collar males between the ages of 18 and 49—drank 80 percent of the beer produced in the country. That meant that every major U.S. brewery had to attract the same customers...or try to reach out to niches not traditionally serviced by the beer industry.

## DIM LITES

One big demographic: people who liked beer, but didn't drink it because it was too high in calories. As sugar-free sodas like Tab and Diet Rite allowed the health-conscious to drink something resembling Coke or Pepsi, several breweries in the mid-1960s began pursuing the idea of low-cal beer.

• In 1964, the Piels Brewing Co. introduced Trommer's Red Letter, "the world's first diet beer." It lasted a comically short six weeks in stores.

• Three years later, Rheingold Brewing Co. of New York introduced a low-cal brew called Gablinger's. Each can was stamped with "Doesn't Fill You Up" and "Contains 99 Calories Less Than Our Regular Beer." Very few beer drinkers (which, again, didn't care if beer made them fat) sampled Gablinger's, which one critic described as "piss with a head."

## LITES OUT

Rheingold withdrew the product and actually gave away the instructions for how to make light beer to a Chicago brewery called Meister Brau. MB

found that the diet beer tasted similar to its flagship Meister Brau, and so launched Meister Brau Lite—in doing so inventing a food and marketing buzzword.

However, MB marketed the beer explicitly as a product for women. Meister Brau Lite

flopped so badly that the company nearly went bankrupt, forcing the brewery's owners to sell to Miller Brewing. Miller planned on discontinuing Meister Brau Lite entirely, until an executive stumbled on a bizarre sales report from the recently acquired company: Meister Brau Lite sold extremely well in Anderson, Indiana, a steel town dominated by the same blue-collar workers who were supposed to hate "diet beer." Why did they like Lite? Curious, the company sent representatives to find out. The consensus was that Lite didn't fill them up as much as regular beers did…enabling them to drink more.

Miller test-marketed "Lite Beer from Miller" in three working-class areas: Springfield, Illinois; Knoxville, Tennessee; and San Diego, California. The result of those tests was that people "can drink more without getting full," which was good, but the beer itself didn't taste so great. In other words, the product would need to be—as its advertising would later claim—"less filling" but "taste great."

## THE RIGHT LITE

Miller president John Murphy decided it was worth a try. He ordered his brewmasters to come up with a beer that tasted like other Miller brands, but still cut the calories per can from around 150 to 96. It took them a little over a year.

Meanwhile, ad people went to work on positioning Lite as a "manly" brew that beer lovers could drink without being ashamed. They decided to build an advertising campaign around professional athletes…except that federal law at the time prohibited using active sports figures to sell alcohol. Miller was stuck.

While riding on a New York City bus, Bob Lenz, the ad executive in charge of Miller's account, came up with the answer. He noticed a poster of former New York Jets star Matt Snell, and it occurred to him that although advertising codes prohibited Miller from using active athletes to sell beer, there was no reason they couldn't employ retired ones. He called Snell.

## LITE BRIGHT

Miller ultimately signed up dozens of ex-athletes for their ad campaign—from baseball players like Boog Powell and Mickey Mantle to bruisers like football's Deacon Jones and hockey's "Boom-Boom" Geoffrion.

As it turned out, using ex-jocks was a master stroke. Because they were a little older (and paunchier) than their active contemporaries, they were easier for beer drinkers to relate to. Plus, they had nothing to prove—they were established heroes. If they said it was okay to drink diet beer, no one was going to argue. And every

TV spot ended with the celebrities heatedly arguing about Lite's best quality—was it that it's "less filling" or that it "tastes great"?—followed by the tagline: "Everything you always wanted in a beer. And less."

## TURN ON THE LITES

When test marketing of Lite exceeded sales projections by an unprecedented 40 percent, it was attributed largely to the advertising campaign. Blue-collar workers not only felt comfortable drinking a light beer, but they also understood that "a third fewer calories" meant that drinking three Lites was only as filling as drinking two regular beers. So rather than cut calories, most Lite drinkers drank more beer, and the sales figures showed it.

Lite was introduced nationally in 1975, and had an astounding effect on the Miller Brewing Co. In 1972 the company was the eighth-largest brewer, selling 5.4 million barrels of beer—compared to number-one Anheuser-Busch's 26.5 million barrels. By 1978—three years after the introduction of Lite—Miller was in second place and gaining, selling approximately 32 million barrels to Anheuser-Busch's 41 million.

# BEER MYTHS, DEBUNKED

**Myth:** Stouts pack substantially more alcohol and calories than other beers. (That's why it's called a "stout.")

**Truth:** Generally, the higher the alcohol content, the higher the calories, because alcohol is very caloric. A 12-ounce serving of Guinness, the world's most famous and best-selling stout, has a relatively low ABV of 4.2 percent, and contains 125 calories. A can of ordinary Budweiser has an ABV of 5 percent and 145 calories.

**Myth:** Guinness is properly served with its famous "two-step" pour.

**Truth:** Here's how it goes: Fill the glass up about three-quarters of the way. Allow the bubbles to subside and settle, and then fill up the glass. It's absolutely unnecessary—just a bit of dramatic, legend-building flourish invented by Guinness's marketing department.

Beer-Topia

**Myth:** Foster's is "Australian for beer."

**Truth:** Foster's was first brewed in Melbourne, Australia, in 1886 by William and Ralph Foster, Irish-American emigrants. It's the second best-selling beer in England, and does respectable business in North America. Foster's, in fact, is almost an entirely exported beer. Despite the famous ad campaign tying Foster's to quintes-sentially Australian things, it's not a big seller in Australia. (The people there prefer Victoria Bitter and Carlton Draught.)

**Myth:** Beer kills brain cells.

**Truth:** Beer make for not smart? That un-possible! Actually, beer—or any alcohol for that matter—does not destroy brain cells. Too much alcohol may temporarily damage the parts of the brain cells responsible for relaying information, which leads to something called "intoxication." They may be out of service for a while, but those brain cells don't go anywhere.

Beer-Topia

# HANGOVERS: HOW DO THEY WORK?

Ben Franklin famously wrote that beer is "proof that God loves us, and loves to see us happy," which sounds lovely until you're kneeling over a toilet at three o'clock in the morning. How can something so delicious hurt us so badly? Science still doesn't really know, but we do seem to be getting closer to figuring out how hangovers happen, and maybe even how to prevent them.

The thoughtful drinker's approach is to stay hydrated by drinking plenty of water between beers, and there's sound science behind that method: Alcohol is a diuretic, a compound that dehydrates the body while also stimulating urine production. However, studies suggest that there actually isn't any connection between dehydration and hangover severity. This isn't to say that we recommend forgoing water while you're out pounding brews, just that it may not be a cure-all.

So if it isn't dehydration, what is it? Scientists now think a hangover may have something to do with a buildup of *acetaldehyde*, a by-product of alcohol that has been found to produce hang-over-like effects (sweating, nausea, hurling) in lab studies. There are also indications that drinking too much can trigger the production of *cytokines*, a signal system the body uses when trying to fight an infection, thus causing some of the familiar fatigue.

The bottom line is that while we don't really know why hangovers happen, we do know this much: As with so many things in life, the best medicine is prevention. Drink reasonably and responsibly, and know and respect your alcoholic limits. Your body will thank you for it...at least until science finally gives us free license to whoop it up.

# BEER MATH

**Gravity:** This distinction has appeared on more and more beers in recent years, but what does it mean? It's a measurement taken throughout the brewing process (with a hydrometer) of a beer's density of fermentable sugars, starting with the wort (original gravity) and ending when the fermentation is complete (final specific gravity). The number printed on the label is the original gravity, minus the final gravity, and then divided by the original gravity. That's the beer's *apparent attentuation*, a measurement of how much fermentation the beer underwent.

**Alcohol by Volume (ABV):** A measurement of the alcohol content of a beer, as calculated by the percentage volume of alcohol. To figure out a beer's ABV, subtract the final gravity from the original gravity and divide by 0.0075.

**Alcohol by Weight (ABW):** This is always lower than ABV. The amount of alcohol in beer measured

according to the percentage weight of alcohol per volume of beer. In other words, 5 percent alcohol by weight equals 5 grams of alcohol per 100 centiliters of beer.

**IBUs:** International Bitterness Units, or points on the scale used to measure a beer's hoppy bitterness. It ranges from the low single digits (light lagers) up to around 100 (Imperial IPAs). Although you might assume that measuring IBUs involves lab workers sitting around downing beer, it's actually a process that centers on solvent extraction to measure *isohumulone*, the acid responsible for hops' bitterness.

**Microbrewery:** More commonly and poetically referred to as a craft brewer, there is a clear definition of what makes a brewery a "microbrewery." According to the Brewers Association (a craft beer trade group), it's a brewery that produces less than 15,000 barrels annually, of which at least 75% is consumed off-site.

# DESTINATION: BEER

**Attraction:** The Beer Can Museum

**Location:** Taunton, Massachusetts

**Details:** It's a museum, and it's full of beer cans.
Not just any cans, mind you—the collection
reaches back and across the annals of beer history.
As curator Kevin Logan puts it, "Many of these
cans tell stories about American and world history
and their values at certain points in time." It isn't
open to the public—tours are by appointment
only or at the annual open house, Museumfest.

**Attraction:** Deutsches
Braureimuseum

**Location:** Munich, Germany

**Details:** This museum offers an
array of exhibits on the evolution
of brewing, including artifacts like
a drinking vessel from 4,000 BC.
There's also a complete microbrewery
on the grounds.

**Attraction:** Brussels Gueze Museum

**Location:** Brussels, Belgium

**Details:** Gueuze, a type of beer that the museum calls "a Brussels specialty from the Middle Ages," is made by blending lambics, a process visitors can witness and learn about while touring the facility. The museum also offers a glimpse of traditional brewing equipment and, more importantly, samples.

**Attraction:** Guinness Storehouse

**Location:** Dublin, Ireland

**Details:** Spread out across seven floors that surround a glass atrium shaped like a pint of Guinness, the massive Storehouse features everything from a close-up look at the ingredients that go into the beer to the history of the company, including its many distinctive ad campaigns. Start at the bottom, work your way to the top, and you'll be rewarded with a visit to the Gravity Bar, which serves Guinness with a panoramic view of Dublin (and a perfect pour).

**Attraction:** The Heineken Experience

**Location:** Amsterdam, the Netherlands

**Details:** Plenty visit Amsterdam to sample an intoxicating substance of a different kind, but there's also this lavish monument to Heinies (and pilsners in general). Located in the original Heineken brewery, built in 1867 and vacated in 1988, it promises "a sensational interactive tour through the dynamic world of Heineken," which is brewspeak for "yes, we have samples."

**Attraction:** Hook Norton Brewery

**Location:** Hook Norton, England

**Details:** Hook Norton offers a case study in the beer version of "if it ain't broke, don't fix it." The brewery's machinery is powered by a steam engine and other equipment that, in most any other brewery, would long ago have been replaced in the name of progress. Very much a working operation, Hook Norton produces cask ale for a network of pubs and grocery outlets, so after you're finished gawking at the brewery's operation, historic

artifacts, and local history exhibits, you can sample a brew that's been produced since 1849.

**Attraction:** National Brewery Centre
**Location:** Burton-upon-Trent, England
**Details:** Formerly the Bass Museum and then the Coors Visitor Center, this museum was dealt a blow in 2008 when Coors opted to shut it down as a cost-cutting measure…in spite of a petition with more than 20,000 supporters' signatures. Fortunately, a local group banded together to explore other options, and in 2010, it reopened as the National Brewery Centre, a tribute not only to Bass but to what the museum refers to as "the social history of the development of brewing," specifically in Burton-upon-Trent. Incorporating a multimedia tour, historic exhibits, and a bar and restaurant serving beer brewed on the site, it also hosts a variety of events; try planning your visit to coincide with the Chili Festival.

**Attraction:** SAB World of Beer

**Location:** Newtown, South Africa

**Details:** This place lives up to its grandiose name with an immersive experience that takes visitors all the way back to beer's beginnings in ancient Egypt. Given that it's hosted by the South African brewing conglomerate SAB, there's an understandable focus on beer's history in the region, including a look at how the company was founded to tap into the burgeoning local demographic of thirsty miners. Visitors may sample malted barley and hops pellets and quaff a couple free pints (and get a free commemorative glass).

**Attraction:** Sapporo Beer Museum

**Location:** Sapporo, Japan

**Details:** Interested in the history of Japanese beer? Start with the nation's only beer museum, located on the former grounds of the Sapporo Sugar Company. The free guided tours offer a glimpse of Sapporo's storied past, including archival ads and marketing materials, as well as historic brewing equipment and a beer garden.

**Attraction:** Tsingtao Beer Museum

**Location:** Shandong, China

**Details:** China's first beer museum pays tribute to more than a century of Tsingtao with a three-part tour: corporate history (from its beginnings as the Chinese branch of the Anglo-German Brewery Co.); how Tsingtao is made today; and the tap-room for samples. It's not entirely dry—the tour includes a trip through the "Drunken House," with slanted walls and floors that reduce even the soberest entrants to stumbling buffoons (as well as video screens for playing back visitors' pratfalls).

**Attraction:** Bruges Beer Museum

**Location:** Bruges, Belgium

**Details:** This one opened in 2014, and it reflects its 21st-century birth with an interactive experience. An iPad-assisted tour allows visitors to walk through at their own pace, and they can use the tablet's camera to scan QR codes that trigger multimedia presentations about the exhibits, which cover the history of beer with a special

concentration on the Belgian brewing tradition. Spread out over three floors, which include beer memorabilia and re-creations of the large foeder drums used to brew Flemish ales, the tour even includes a "children's version" of the museum.

**Attraction:** A. Le Coq Beer Museum
**Location:** Tartu, Estonia
**Details:** Estonia probably isn't one of the first places that come to mind when you think about beer, but that might change after you have the unique privilege of whiling away a couple of hours at the nexus of Baltic brewing. In addition to a tour of the A. Le Coq Brewery, the museum houses hundreds of years of history in an old malt drying tower. Guided tours take two hours, and, as with just about every other stop on our world beer museum map, include samples of the product.

**Attraction:** National Brewery Museum

**Location:** Potosi, Wisconsin

**Details:** The Potosi Brewing Company actually houses a pair of museums: the National Brewery Museum, which pays tribute to "the rich history of America's breweries" with exhibits and an assortment of memorabilia, and the Potosi Brewing Company Transportation Museum, which frames the brewery's history through its use of waterways and roadways. It's the former attraction that will probably be of most interest to beer aficionados, and for good reason—after an extensive rebuilding and remodeling campaign that found new owner Gary David spearheading efforts to restore the historic (and long-defunct) PBC building, the museum houses an extensive collection that includes noteworthy bottles, cans, ads, and other assorted beer memorabilia.

# BEERS FROM TV

• Indiana's Federation of Beer, a brewery named for the United Federation of Planets from *Star Trek*, makes a beer called Roggen Dunkel. It's inspired by a potent tipple consumed by the fearsome Klingons on *Star Trek: The Next Generation*. It's made with sweet and rye malts with notes of banana and cloves.

• In 2014, Philadelphia's Dock Street Brewery introduced Dock Street Walker—"walkers" are what characters call zombies on *The Walking Dead*. Colored with cranberries to make it bloodred, it's also brewed with smoked goat braaaaains.

• New York brewery Ommegang makes three beers inspired by HBO's *Game of Thrones*: Iron Throne Ale, Take the Black Stout, and Fire and Blood Red Ale. "Fire and Blood" is the motto of Daenerys Targaryen, "the mother of dragons." Each bottle depicts one of three different dragons.

*Beer-Topia*

# "HOORAY BEER!"

*Match the classic ad slogan to the beer it promoted.*
*Answers are on page 254.*

**1.** "The beer that made Milwaukee famous"

**2.** "The champagne of bottled beers"

**3.** "The beer refreshing"

**4.** "Tap the Rockies"

**5.** "I am Canadian!"

**6.** "Hooray beer!"

**7.** "Miles away from ordinary"

**8.** "The king of beers"

**9.** "You never forget your first girl"

**10.** "Head for the mountains"

**11.** "Reassuringly expensive"

**12.** "Refreshes your spirit"

**13.** "Life beckons"

**14.** "Australian for beer"

**15.** "It works every time"

**16.** "The beer to have when you're having more than one"

**17.** "Reach for greatness"

**18.** "America's world class beer"

**a)** Coors

**b)** Old Milwaukee

**c)** Stella Artois

**d)** Beck's

**e)** Shaefer

**f)** Colt .45

**g)** Molson

**h)** Corona

**i)** Hamm's

**j)** Courage

**k)** Foster's

**19.** "This one has the touch"

**20.** "It's what your right arm is for"

**21.** "It just doesn't get any better than this"

**l)** High Life

**m)** Schlitz

**n)** Bass Ale

**o)** Samuel Adams

**p)** Busch

**q)** Guinness

**r)** St. Pauli Girl

**s)** Budweiser

**t)** Red Stripe

**u)** Pabst Blue Ribbon

# THIS BUD(S) FOR YOU

*Three distinctly different brews from three different eras all claim to be the one true Budweiser. Which Bud's the true brew?*

• Ceské Budejovice, a city in what is now the Czech Republic, is commonly known by its German name, Budweis. Breweries have operated there since the 13th century, and in 1795, a group of German residents opened a new one, Budweiser Bier Bürgerbräu. Their signature beer was a light-colored, mild German-style lager they called Budweiser (or "of Budweis").

• In the late 1860s, American brewer Adolphe Busch was looking for ways to improve the quality and shelf life of the beers being made at the St. Louis brewery he co-owned with his father-in-law, Eberhard Anheuser—mostly dark ales, which were the most popular style at the time. Busch toured Europe, studying brewing methods and

sampling many different types of beer. His favorite was the one he drank in Budweis: Budweiser. In 1876, Busch's brewery developed a beer similar to Budweiser to sell in the United States, and he called it…Budweiser. On the strength of that beer, Anheuser-Busch became America's biggest beermaker in less than 20 years.

• In 1895, King William II of Württemberg (today a part of Germany) made Bürgerbräu's Budweiser his official court beer. With William's endorsement, Bürgerbräu's sales skyrocketed. Result: A group of enterprising brewers decided to cash 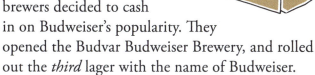 in on Budweiser's popularity. They opened the Budvar Budweiser Brewery, and rolled out the *third* lager with the name of Budweiser.

Around 1900, the two Budweis-based Budweiser breweries learned that Busch's version of Budweiser was selling extremely well in the United States. Both Bürgerbräu and Budvar began exporting their Budweisers to America. That put three different beers called Budweiser—all of which were technically very similar—into the U.S. marketplace. This didn't lead to consumer confusion. Reason: There was a lot more of Busch's Budweiser in stores—by a ratio of 10 to 1.

It all came to a head in 1901 at a brewing-industry trade fair attended by representatives from all three breweries. The parties met...and argued about which was the real Budweiser and who should get the rights to the very lucrative and very recognizable brand name. The Bürgerbräu brewers argued that they should have the rights to "Budweiser" because they made their lagers in Budweis, and they'd been doing it since 1795. Anheuser-Busch representatives contended that they owned the North American trademark on the Budweiser name and had the paperwork to prove it.

A 10-year courtroom battle ensued. In 1911, they reached an agreement: Each brewer could continue to use the name Budweiser, but only in certain territories. Anheuser-Busch was granted the right to sell its Budweiser in North America only. The two European brewers agreed to share the name and the European market. The two breweries kept a tenuous peace for another few years, until the conclusion of World War I, when both operations were seized by the Czech government.

The Bürgerbräu brewers were expelled to Germany. And because Germany's armies had

ravaged much of Europe, the name "Budweiser" became loathed there, leading the Czech government to ban the name altogether. The new operators of the Bürgerbräu brewery began selling their beer under names

like "Crystal" and "Samson." The owners of the Budvar brewery had no choice but to drop the Budweiser name. They renamed their beer Budejovický Budvar.

The three breweries kept out of each other's hair, all the way to the 1990s. By then, Anheuser-Busch had become one of the world's largest brewers and was selling its Budweiser lager all across Europe, but under the name "Bud" to avoid another round of legal bickering. After the fall of communism in Czechoslovakia and the creation of the Czech Republic in 1993, the Budvar and Bürgerbräu breweries decided to start selling beer under the name "Budweiser" again.

That led to another round of complex legal entanglements and a bitter dispute among the three breweries that continues to this day. You can find any of these three lagers all across Europe and North America, but depending on your exact location, they might be called something else.

# A BEER MIXTAPE

- Two Nice Girls, "I Spent My Last $10 (On Birth Control and Beer)" (1989)

- Bob Wills and the Texas Playboys, "Bubbles in My Beer" (1947)

- Tom Waits, "Warm Beer, Cold Women" (1975)

- The Replacements, "Beer for Breakfast" (1987)

- Bessie Smith, "Gimme a Pigfoot (And a Bottle of Beer)" (1933)

- Jacques Brel, "La Bière" (1968)

- Ernest Neubach and Ralph Maria Siegel, "In Heaven There Is No Beer" (1956)

- Captain Beefheart, "Long Neck Bottles" (1972)

- The Andrews Sisters, "Beer Barrel Polka" (1939)

- Memphis Slim, "Beer Drinking Woman" (1940)

- Billy Currington, "Pretty Good at Drinking Beer" (2010)

- Reel Big Fish, "Beer" (1995)

- The Clancy Brothers, "Beer Beer Beer" (1970)

- Black Flag, "Six Pack" (1981)

- The Dubliners, "Pub with No Beer" (1967)

- ZZ Top, "Beer Drinkers and Hell Raisers" (1973)

- Tom T. Hall, "I Like Beer" (1975)

- "John Barleycorn" (Traditional British folk song)

- Johnny Cash, "I Hardly Ever Sing Beer Drinking Songs" (1975)

# THE UNITED STATES OF BEER, PART 3

**Maine:** For many, "Maine beer" is synonymous with Allagash, the forward-thinking Portland brewery that helped popularize Belgian-style beer in the U.S. The brewery's other offerings include Merveilleux, a barrel-aged wild ale. But Allagash is far from alone in the Pine Tree State; any list of Maine's best breweries would be incomplete without a mention of the Maine Beer Company, whose Dinner and Lunch brews are among the most highly sought-after.

**Maryland:** Flying Dog in Frederick is probably the best-known here. Its brash and flavorful aesthetic is reflected in its distinctive, Ralph Steadman–inspired gonzo packaging. Baltimore's Stillwater Artisanal, however, might be gearing up to give Flying Dog a run for its money; their Gose Gone Wild and barrel-aged brews are among the best-reviewed in the state.

**Massachusetts:** Visit any bar in New England, and you'll find Sam Adams on tap, but Massachusetts is also home to a long list of quality craft brews. Many of these are offered by Ipswich's Clown Shoes Beer, an irreverent bunch whose fun and aggressive approach to brewing is apparent in offerings like their Very Angry Beast, Undead Party Crasher, and Luchador en Fuego Imperial Stouts.

**Michigan:** A person could get lost in the incredible beers offered by Bells Brewery in Galesburg and Founders Brewing Company in Grand Rapids, which include the best stouts in Michigan (Bells Black Note Stout and Founders Kentucky Breakfast Stout are particularly amazing) as well as one of the best IPAs you can find (Bells Two Hearted Ale) and one whopper of a Scotch Ale (Founders Backwoods Bastard). Looking for something a little different? Kuhnhenn Brewing in Warren makes an unforgettable Bourbon Barrel French Toast Mead.

Beer-Topia

**Minnesota:** The quirky city of Minneapolis loves its craft beer, and the best-loved of them all might be those by Surly Brewing Company. So popular that they had to pull their beer from outside markets for three years in order to fully serve hometown consumers, the folks at SBC were rewarded with the passage of legislation undoing a Prohibition-era ban on establishments making and selling their beer in the same location, thus clearing the way for a multimillion-dollar Surly "destination brewery" and pub. Start off with their Abrasive Ale, a double IPA named in honor of the founder's parents, who operated the sandpaper factory where Surly eventually started brewing.

**Mississippi:** Lazy Magnolia Brewing Company in Klin makes really, really great beer. Start off with their Timber Beast Imperial Rye Pale Ale and work your way down the line.

**Missouri:** Since 1989, St. Louis's craft brewing scene has proudly played host to Boulevard Brewing Company, and even though they're no

Beer-Topia

longer independently owned—Belgium's Duvel-Moortgat purchased a majority stake in 2013—Boulevard's line still rates among the best craft beer you can find in the home state of Budweiser.

**Montana:** Modern beer enthusiasts have so many craft-brewed options that we've been trained to think that the best stuff is usually made by the smallest companies, but sometimes, biggest is best—just look at Missoula's Big Sky Brewing Company, sellers of Montana's most popular (and most widely distributed) suds. Established in 1995, Big Sky's core lineup is small, led by its Moose Drool Brown Ale, Scape Goat Pale Ale, Big Sky IPA, Powder Hound Winter Ale, Summer Honey Seasonal Ale, and Trout Slayer Ale. But it also produces a number of renowned limited brews, including the Ivan the Terrible barrel-aged imperial stout and Olde Bluehair Barleywine.

**Nebraska:** Founded in 2007 in La Vista, the Nebraska Brewing Company produces much of the state's best-reviewed beers, led by a Reserve

Series lineup that includes its excellent Black Betty Russian Imperial Stout and a barrel-aged version of its HopAnomaly Belgian Strong Ale. And they may not be strictly regional for long: In early 2014, Nebraska Brewing moved into a larger facility big enough to allow for up to 1.5 million gallons of annual production.

**Nevada:** The Silver State has its share of craft breweries, the biggest and oldest of which is Great Basin Brewing Company, established in Sparks in 1993. Joseph James and Big Dog's are among Great Basin's younger competitors, but the fastest growing of the bunch might be Tenaya Creek Brewery in Las Vegas, which plans a major expansion close to the Strip in early 2015—so much the better for fans of its Imperial Stout, War Dog Imperial IPA, and Old Jackalope Barleywine.

*For part 4 of the story, turn to page 225.*

Beer-Topia

# FUNNY (AND REAL) BRITISH PUB NAMES

The Leg of Mutton and Cauliflower

The Duke Without a Head

Bull and Spectacles

Donkey on Fire

Dirty Dick's

The Jolly Taxpayer

Ye Olde Trip to Jerusalem

Cow and Snuffers

The Thatcher's Foot

Muscular Arms

The Sociable Plover

The Spinner and Bergamot

The Strawberry Duck

Who'd A Thought It

Sally Up Steps

Volunteer Rifleman Corps Inn

The Quiet Woman

The Old Queen's Head

Beer-Topia

Round of Carrots

The Inn Next Door
Burnt Down

The Bucket of Blood

The Poosy Nancies

The Blind Beggar

The Olde Cheshire
Cheese

The Bitter End

Q

Ye Olde Fighting
Cocks

The Crooked House

Slug and Lettuce

The Dying Cow

The Old New Inn

The Case Is Altered

The Same Yet

The
Penny-Come-Quick

Ye Olde Bung Hole

The Ram Jam

The Chocolate Poodle

The Drunken Duck

The House Without a
Name

The Fool & Bladder

# WEIGHTS & MEASURES

**Bomber.** Also known as a "tallboy," this is a beer sold in a 22-ounce bottle.

**Growler.** A big, capped glass jug of beer, holding around 64 ounces. Legend says that they got their name because they used to be covered pails, and as the carbon dioxide burped its way out from under the lid, it made a "growling" noise.

**Barrel.** In the U.S., a barrel holds 31.5 gallons. In the UK, a barrel holds 36 imperial gallons. (British barrels, obviously, are better.)

**Keg.** A keg is a container holding half a barrel, or 15.5 gallons. A half-keg is commonly referred to as a pony keg.

**Hogshead.** A cooler way of saying "cask that holds 54 imperial gallons," roughly 64 U.S. gallons.

# THE GOATS WHO LOVED BEER

Lajitas is a tiny town of fewer than 200 people in West Texas, where the only major business is a store called The Trading Post. Residing there is Clay Henry Moore III, the town's most prominent citizen. Like his father and grandfather, Clay Henry Moore III is the mayor of Lajitas. Also like his father and grandfather, he's a goat that drinks beer all day.

In the 1980s, the first Clay Henry Moore became a tourist attraction when the proprietors of The Trading Post put him out front, luring tourists to watch the goat's amazing "talent" of guzzling dozens of Lone Star longnecks every day. (The Trading Post, it should be noted, sells beer.) In a ceremonial move in 1986, the tiny town elected Clay its mayor, a position he held until his death in 1992. Cause of death: He got into a drunken brawl with his son, Clay Henry Moore

Jr., who had also been taught to drink beer. They literally butted heads over a lady goat they both wanted to mate with. (Seriously.)

Recalling a Shakespearean tragedy, Clay Henry Moore Jr. ascended to power and inherited his father's other job of beer-drinking tourist attraction. This goat drank 35 to 40 beers a day, much less than his father, but he still managed to book an appearance on *The Sally Jesse Raphael Show* in 1995.

Continuing the dynasty, Clay Henry Moore III is the current mayor and official beer goat of Lajitas. In 2002, there was an assassination attempt. Local resident Jim Bob Hargrove castrated the goat…because tourists were feeding him beer on a Sunday, forbidden by local blue laws. Clay made a full recovery.

However, in 2014, he nearly lost his mayoral post to an upstart candidate, Pancho…a beer-drinking donkey.

# YOUR DAD'S BEER, PART 2

*More profiles of some enduring beer labels.*
*(Part 1 starts on page 137.)*

**Sam Adams:** This one isn't as old as you think it is. It's the flagship label of the Boston Beer Company, a partnership founded in 1984, when the craft beer movement was in its infancy. Although the first batches were made in co-founder Jim Koch's home, he and his partners, Harry Rubin and Lorenzo Lamadrid, were all Harvard guys with advanced degrees. They each played to their separate strengths, carving out market share at a time when American beer drinkers bought little besides Miller Lite and Budweiser.

It helped that the company brewed beer that people actually wanted to drink, as reflected by the splashy showing they made at the Great

American Beer Festival in 1985—Samuel Adams Boston Lager took top honors and quickly set Boston Beer Company on a fast path to profitability. Just four years later, Koch and his partners had moved 63,000 barrels of Sam Adams.

In recent years, Boston Beer has risen to compete with Yuengling for the title of largest American-owned brewing company, and it's become one of the dependable defaults for drinkers who don't want Bud, but don't want an overly hoppy microbrew either. The company has also widely expanded its offerings, adding a growing list of seasonal brews as well as an IPA and its Utopias series, which is not for those with faint palates or slender bankrolls (see page 135).

**Iron City:** Founded in 1861 by German immigrant Edward Frauenheim, Iron City

Brewery quickly became a fixture in Pittsburgh's Lawrenceville neighborhood, where Frauenheim built a distinctive brick brewhouse in 1866—one of the first in a series of aggressive expansions that soon helped make Iron City the biggest brewery in Pittsburgh.

Frauenheim's thirst for growth left the company with one of the more impressive brewing facilities in the country. His decision to take part in the 1899 mega-merger that created the Pittsburgh Brewing Company helped shield him and his business partners from the heavy attrition of Prohibition, which the company coped with by selling everything from ice cream to soda. With those lean years behind it, PBC continued to expand, purchasing additional assets and adjusting its offerings to meet consumers' changing demands—as they did in the late 1970s, cornering the regional light beer market with IC Light.

Iron City fell victim to softening demand and the vagaries of corporate whims in later years.

Between the mid-1980s and mid-1990s, PBC changed hands more than once. By 2005, PBC found itself in bankruptcy court. In 2007, PBC was purchased yet again, given back its old Iron City Brewing Company name, and, as of 2009, bottling at the old Latrobe Brewing Company plant where Rolling Rock was once produced.

**Guinness:** Guinness is definitely not the sort of blue-collar brew a fellow is apt to imbibe in great quantities after a hard day at work—especially these days, given that the stout comes in cans fitted with gas cartridges that are supposed to replicate the draught experience. Regardless, it's a beer steeped in tradition.

First offered in 1759 by Irish brewer Arthur Guinness, it's arguably the world's best-loved stout. Modern drinkers might hasten to steer you in the direction of any one of a number of beers that offer more unusual or flavorful takes on the variety, but none of them boasts the one-of-a-kind experience that Guinness pilgrims get when

venturing to the company's facility at St. James's Gate in Dublin—which savvy Arthur Guinness agreed to lease for 9,000 years for the annual fee of £45.

Of course, the company eventually bought the land, as well as a substantial portion of the land around St. James's Gate, which once served as the location for corporate housing and a company-built power plant. All that muscle mostly went into the production of more dry stout. Although Guinness has offered a small assortment of additional brews, including the incongruous Guinness Blonde American Lager, it'll always be known for that old standby. When someone says "Guinness," it's the stout that comes to mind, not the company.

And for good reason: While other breweries have explored and innovated the stout, Guinness

has focused on doing one thing extremely well—to the point that the company recommends an exact pouring method (it's supposed to take you 119.5 seconds to deliver the perfect Guinness pour) and a specific glass, which is designed according to strict (albeit continually changing) guidelines.

That singular dedication has helped insulate Guinness from a lot of the corporate shenanigans that plagued their peers, although not entirely; in 1997, the company merged with Grand Metropolitan, creating the British beverage conglomerate Diageo, a massive spirits emporium whose assets include Smirnoff, Baileys, and Johnnie Walker, any one of which, now that we think about it, might be accurately described as Your Dad's Booze.

# RUNNING ON BEER

• Since 2005, the California brewer Sierra Nevada has had its own fuel cell–based and ultra-clean electric power plant right inside its brewery. It originally ran on piped-in natural gas, but as of 2006, it runs on a mix of natural gas and methane, a by-product of the water-treatment process that the brewery uses. So the more beer they brew, the more methane they produce and the less natural gas they use.

• City Brewery of La Crosse, Wisconsin, generates a lot of biogas waste product from making beer. How much? About three million kilowatt-hours' worth of annual electricity. Captured, cleaned, and dispersed through a special engine called a jenbacher, the energy goes straight down the street to the Gundersen Lutheran Health System. The vast majority of the hospital's energy needs are provided by City Brewery.

Beer-Topia

# PILGRIM PRIDE

We tend to think of the Pilgrims as an austere and sober bunch, but that's largely a fallacy imposed after the fact by folks in more temperate times. In reality, the passengers on board the *Mayflower* were in mostly equal parts religious separatists, those there for a New World–sized paycheck, and crew members and servants.

They set sail in August of 1620 and dropped into New England just in time for winter. There were a number of problems with this, one of them being that the ship was supposed to land in Virginia. In fact, where the *Mayflower* ultimately landed was roughly a degree of latitude north of the area where they'd been granted license to start a plantation. So why did they do it? They were also out of beer.

It's true. In *Mourt's Relation*, a journal of the voyage written by colonists Edward Winslow and William Bradford, one entry states that the ship had opted to dock in what they called "Thievish Harbor," a.k.a. Plymouth Bay, because, in their words, "We could not now take time for further search or consideration, our victuals being much spent, especially our beer, and it being now the 19th of December."

\*    \*    \*

## 8 SLANG TERMS FOR BEER

**1.** Amber nectar

**2.** Barley pop

**3.** Brewski

**4.** Cold coffee

**5.** Laughing water

**6.** Liquid bread

**7.** Suds

**8.** Vitamin B

# EVERYTHING'S FINING

*Finings are nonessential ingredients added during the brewing process to clarify a beer's appearance, or to add a hint of flavor. Let's hope you can't taste any of these finings in your beer, all of which are really used by big brewers, craft brewers, and homebrewers alike.*

• **Irish moss**...which is seaweed

• **Whirlfloc**, or seaweed in concentrated tablet form, with extra carrageenan (the "active ingredient" in seaweed)

• **Silica gel**

• **Polycar**...which is powdered, nontoxic plastic

• **Casein**, a milk protein

• **Albumen**, otherwise known as egg whites

• **Isinglass**, a gelatin made from dried fish bladders. There's isinglass in every glass of Guinness.

# THE WORLD'S TOP BEERHOUNDS

**Michael Jackson.** The mighty Jackson, whose groundbreaking work as a beer and whiskey critic (nice work if you can get it, right?) produced not only the seminal series *The Beer Hunter* as well as a long list of beloved best-sellers, but entirely new ways of looking at a beer, both in its proper cultural context and its place in the pantheon of brewing styles. None of these things were given much serious thought before Jackson started writing in the 1970s. Jackson died in 2007, but his legacy lives on with the craft brew movement and books like this one.

**Wade Boggs.** Even in the context of the same sport that gave us Hall of Fame sluggers/imbibers like Babe Ruth and Mickey Mantle, Boggs was a guy who always had either a beer or a baseball in his hand. H reportedly once downed more than 60 cans of Miller Lite on a cross-country flight.

**Paul Behan.** On March 16, 2001, Behan appeared on the *Virgin Radio Breakfast* talk show in England and set a new speed record for drinking a pint of Guinness. (It's literally a Guinness world record!) He polished it off in just 3.9 seconds… although Behan insisted that he could do better, claiming a private personal best of 1.5 seconds.

**Angelo Cammarata.** What would our pursuit of beer be without those who serve it to us? Among that holy order, none served longer than the proprietor of the Pennsylvania's Cammarata's Cafe, who opened his taps as soon as Prohibition ended at the stroke of midnight on April 7, 1933…and kept right on serving patrons until 2009, when his sons decided to sell the place because they thought they were too old to effectively manage the business. A spry 95 when he retired, Cammarata was profiled in Playboy, appeared on *The Daily Show*, and was honored by Jim Beam, who enshrined him in their Bartender Hall of Fame.

# BEER MEETS CAFFEINE

After watching all the cool club kids order millions of Red Bull and vodka cocktails in the early 2000s, the beer industry decided to try and get in on the action by launching brews that combined higher alcohol volume with stimulants, such as caffeine, ginseng, and guarana.

Some drinks, like Miller's Sparks and Budweiser's Tilt, came in the same Day-Glo flavors as your average Smirnoff Ice and were packaged in giant, brightly colored, oversized cans. For those who prefer that their beerlike energy drink taste like beer, there was Bud Extra, a 6.6% ABV concoction marketed with posters bearing the slogan "Go longer."

America's brief foray into energy beer ended when a brigade of party-pooping state attorneys general pressured bottlers to stop making them because mixing alcohol with caffeine tends to

result in stuff like injuries, illness, and blackouts. (They also accused the companies of marketing the fruity drinks to minors.) These days, Sparks, Tilt, and newer entries like Joose and Four Loko are just good old-fashioned high-alcohol beverages that come in flavors like Blue Raspberry and Green Apple—which counts as a happy ending because everyone knows fruit is good for you.

\*    \*    \*

## GREASE IS THE WORD

Whether it's plate of poutine in Canada, or a box of Dunkin' Donuts in the U.S., there's one thing many drinkers are drawn to "the morning after," and that's a heaping mound of fatty food. There may not be much medical basis to it—doctors suggest that by the time you're feeling hungover, it's too late for the grease to absorb enough alcohol to improve your state—but who cares? When you end a night of overindulgence with eggs and bacon, we're calling that a win-win.

# THE UNITED STATES OF BEER, PART 4

**New Hampshire:** Hampton's Smuttynose Brewing Company has been the granddaddy of Granite State craft breweries since it started bottling in 1994. A standout is their Baltic Porter. The competition includes Hampton's Blue Lobster Brewing Company, White Birch Brewing in Hooksett, and the Stoneface Brewing Company in Newington, which bottles a great IPA.

**New Jersey:** Travelers touching down at Newark International Airport are greeted with the sight of a giant Anheuser-Busch bottling plant. But the Garden State has birthed a bumper crop of craft brewery selections since the mid-1990s, including Kane Brewing Company's Kane Held High IPA, Flying Fish's Exit 9 American Strong Ale, and the wacky beers bottled by Carton Brewing, such as their Intermezzo green apple wasabi root sour ale and Monkey Chased the Weasel Berliner weiss.

Beer-Topia

**New Mexico:** A decade ago, there were five breweries statewide, but it's a rapidly expanding business in the Land of Enchantment. Notable exports include La Cumbre's Elevated IPA, Marble Brewery's Imperial Red Ale, and the Imperial Java Stout offered by Santa Fe Brewing Company.

**New York:** Long before Brooklyn became trendy, the borough hosted one of the region's finest microbreweries. Founded in 1987, Brooklyn Brewery offers some of the better beer made in the city. Also intriguing are some of the state's upstarts, like Lakewood's Southern Tier Brewing Company and its array of session stuff, including its 422 Pale Wheat Ale and Eurotrash Pilz, as well as eyebrow-raising limited runs such as its must-have Creme Brulee Stout.

**North Carolina:** Solid options include the Event Horizon Imperial Stout from the Olde Hickory Brewery and the Bourbon Barrel Milk Stout from Duck-Rabbit Craft Brewery. The rising star in the Tarheel State is Foothills Brewing in

Winston-Salem, not only because they make excellent beer—the Sexual Chocolate Imperial Stout is worthy of its name—but also because it was started by a husband-and-wife duo. The couple that brews together, stays together!

**North Dakota:** North Dakota is the nation's leader in barley production, which makes it a natural breeding ground for terrific beer. Find a tap dispensing some of Fargo Brewing Company's offerings, which include the Iron Horse Pale Ale and Sod Buster Porter. In the mood for a North Dakota IPA? Seek out Feast Like a Sultan from the Laughing Sun Brewing Company in Bismarck.

**Ohio:** A sudsy cornucopia flows forth from Hoppin' Frog Brewery, the brainchild of Akron's Fred Karm. Since 2006, Karm has been cheering Buckeye Staters with pints of B.O.R.I.S. and D.O.R.I.S. Imperial Stouts, as well as its Mean Manalishi Double IPA and a handful of fruit-flavored brews.

**Oklahoma:** Chase and Colin Healey founded Prairie Artisan Ales in 2012, and successfully crowdfunded the completion of a brewhouse dedicated to barrel-aged beer. They hit the ground running: According to RateBeer.com users, nine of the Sooner State's top 10 beers are made by Prairie Artisan.

**Oregon:** Oregon is arguably the craft beer capital of the world, in terms of both production and consumption—in 2013, it led the U.S. in breweries per capita and dollars spent on craft beer. Discerning drinkers are familiar with some of the state's better-known wares, including those bottled by Rogue Ales and Full Sail Brewing Company. But for a good Beaver State brew, it's hard to go wrong with Hair of the Dog, a 20-year-old company known for aggressive flavors and high ABVs.

**Pennsylvania:** You can't talk about Pennsylvania beer without mentioning Yuengling, the oldest-operating brewing company in the U.S. For some, Yuengling is a drinking experience worth crossing

state lines to achieve; for others, it's simply a decent, moderately priced beer. Either way, your Keystone State bar travels should probably include at least a glass of the stuff (which you can order in Pennsylvania simply by asking for a lager) and then branch out into some of the tasty craft-brewed selections offered by local companies like Tröegs, Tired Hands, Bullfrog, and Victory.

**Rhode Island:** Ocean State beer is historically synonymous with the Narragansett Brewing Company. Formerly the biggest brewing company in New England, Narragansett fell on hard times during the 1970s and 1980s, but it's undergone a renaissance in recent years since the rights to the label were purchased by a team of local investors. The core of the company's line is solid, drink-able, undemanding stuff sold in tallboy cans, but they also offer a few locally craft-brewed options, including their eagerly anticipated holiday brew, Autocrat Coffee Milk Stout.

*For part 5, turn to page 243.*

# 8 ODD BEER LAWS

**Texas:** Drinking more than three sips of beer while standing up is technically against the law.

**Alaska:** It's illegal to give beer to a moose.

**Colorado:** Drinking on horseback? That's a crime.

**Utah:** It's against the law to serve liquor or Arbor Day.

**Hawaii:** Whistling in a bar is illegal.

**Massachusetts:** "Happy hour" is prohibited.

**Oklahoma:** Beer with an ABV of more than 4 percent cannot be sold chilled.

**Cedar City, Utah:** If your shoelaces are untied while you're drinking a beer? That's illegal.

Beer-Topia

# BEAR-TOPIA

Hamm's was a major beer brand in the mid-20th century, and a lot of that is due to a massively popular ad campaign. Dozens of animated ads starred an unnamed, chubby black-and-white bear. He'd play a sport, like baseball or logrolling, inevitably lose due to his own mistakes or clumsiness, and take it in stride with a goofy grin. The ads always took place in the natural wilds of Hamm's home state of Minnesota, reflected in the memorable, drum-driven jingle: "From the land of sky blue waters / from the land of pines, lofty balsams / comes the beer refreshing / Hamm's the beer refreshing."

Hamm's Brewery hired Minneapolis ad agency Campbell Mithun in 1952 to launch its first TV campaign. Based on a napkin sketch given to him by executive Cleo Hoval, staff artist Patrick DesJarlait created the friendly bear. The cartoon ads were produced by former Disney animator

Howard Smith and debuted in 1953—the first ever animated spokes-creature to advertise beer.

Airing first only in Minnesota, the cartoon ads featuring the silent bear and the memorable jingle (based on Rudolf Friml's classical piece "Natoma," with drums provided by the ad agency's Ray Mithun banging on empty tuna cans) soon went national. Hamm's became the biggest beer sponsor of sports on TV and radio in the 1960s, with specially made Bear ads for football and baseball teams in Minneapolis, Chicago, Kansas City, California, Texas, and Wisconsin. A 1965 poll named the Hamm's Bear the most-liked ad mascot in the country, a tremendous feat given that the ads only aired in 31 states.

Not wanting to wear out its welcome, Hamm's tried to retire the character several times in the late 1960s and 1970s. But every time they did,

they received complaints, and sales plummeted. So the Bear stayed, starring in ads well until the 1980s. They petered out by 1990. By that time, Pabst owned Hamm's, and feared being accused of using the animated bear as a ploy to market alcohol to children.

And yet, the Hamm's Bear lived on. The bear appeared on hundreds of different pieces of glassware, trays, mirrors, and other promotional merchandise in the 1960 and 1970s, which enjoys a robust collector's market. The Hamm's Club, which collects and trades Bear gear, was responsible for erecting a statue of the Bear in 2005 at St. Paul's Seventh Street Mall. Around the same time, *Ad Age* named the campaign one of the best of the 20th century. The *St. Paul Pioneer Press* went one better in 2000, naming the goofy bear one of the most influential Minnesotans of all time.

# THE LONDON BEER FLOOD

The London Beer Flood was not nearly as much fun as it might sound. The Horse Shoe Brewery on Tottenham Court Road suffered a vat failure in October 1814 that unleashed a 15-foot-high torrent of porter through the city streets, scaring and confusing countless Londoners and ultimately resulting in the deaths of eight people.

Particularly problematic was the fact that the flood gushed into St. Giles Rookery, a slum whose soon-to-be-beer-filled basements were home to entire families whose lives were upended in an instant by the equivalent of 9,000 errant barrels.

Prohibition may not have convinced most people to stop drinking, but we're betting anyone who had to deal with the aftereffects of a house flooded with beer probably wasn't in any hurry to raise a glass after the mess dried out.

# CANADIAN BEER COCKTAILS

*Canadians love their beer so much that they mix all sorts of weird stuff into that Molson or Labatt's.*

**Drink:** Clam Eye

**Ingredients:** Beer, Clamato, celery salt, Tabasco, Worcestershire sauce

**Details:** The Caesar is the Canadian take on the Bloody Mary, substituting clam-and-tomato juice for the plain tomato juice. The Clam Eye is a beered-up version of the Caesar, with beer replacing the vodka.

**Drink:** Camel Piss

**Ingredients:** Beer, tequila, dark rum, ouzo, anise liqueur, Mountain Dew

**Details:** We assume this gets its name from its yellow color and strength.

**Drink:** Canadian Car Bomb
**Ingredients:** Beer, whisky
**Details:** This take on the Irish Car Bomb is authentically made with Canadian beer and Canadian whisky.

**Drink:** Porch Climber
**Ingredients:** Beer, pink lemonade, vodka, whisky
**Details:** So named because it will leave you climbing back onto the porch after you've fallen off it after a couple of these. (A version made with Sprite is called "Skip and Go Naked.")

**Drink:** Flaming Engineer
**Ingredients:** Beer, Amaretto, whisky, orange juice
**Details:** For relief from their rigorous studies, engineering students at Ryerson University in Toronto designed this special drink.

# THE PERFECT POUR

*A step-by-step guide.*

**1.** Choose the appropriate glass (see page 31). Make sure it's clean of oils and sediment. Those things are gross, and they alter the taste of a beer.

**2.** Rest the edge of the bottom on a flat surface and tilt the glass to about a 45-degree angle. Hold it firmly.

**3.** Hold the bottle or can an inch or two above the rim of the glass. (This keeps the rim, where you'll place your lips, clean.)

**4.** Pour in a rapid, steady stream down the side of the glass. When the glass is half-full, slowly angle the glass so it's back upright. This will give the beer a nice head.

**5.** Wait a few seconds for the head to settle. Enjoy!

Beer-Topia

# CAN'T GET ENOUGH OF THAT WONDERFUL DUFF

*Crack open an imaginary cold one and try to match these fictitious brews to the movie, book, or TV show that served them. (Answers on page 254.)*

**1.** Shotz Beer

**2.** Romulan Ale

**3.** Pawtucket Patriot

**4.** Panther Pilsner

**5.** Black Death Malt Liquor

**6.** Wharmpess Beer

**7.** Schraderbrau

**8.** Ent Draught

**9.** Old Dusseldorf

**10.** Lobrau

**11.** Butterbeer

**12.** Alamo Beer

**13.** Elsinore Beer

**14.** Spice Beer

**15.** Buzz Beer

**16.** "Beer"

**17.** Duff

a) *South Park*

b) *Magnum, P.I.*

c) *Breaking Bad*

d) *The Drew Carey Show*

e) *Strange Brew*

f) *The Simpsons*

g) *Dune*

h) *Futurama*

i) *Harry Potter*

j) *WKRP in Cincinnati*

k) *The Three Stooges*

l) *Family Guy*

m) *The Lord of the Rings*

n) *Star Trek*

o) *Laverne and Shirley*

p) *How I Met Your Mother*

q) *King of the Hill*

# THE DRY BEER FAD

Soon after the successful introduction into Japan of "dry" beers in the 1980s, the American beer industry jumped into dry beer, too. **How exactly can a liquid be dry?** In the case of beer, it's a brew with more carbonation and less aftertaste, giving an overall "crisper" or "dryer" mouthfeel.

Bud Dry employed a massive rollout ad campaign ("Why ask why? Try Bud Dry"), and for a few years, drinkers could and did frequently choose "dry" brews from most of the major companies. By 1995, however, the fad had faded. Budweiser shifted its marketing focus to the new Bud Ice, which used freeze-distilling to produce a brew with slightly higher alcohol content, discovering that fuzzy, amorphous concepts like "flavor" and "aftertaste" really don't matter when you're giving your customers a new product that will get them drunk more efficiently.

Beer-Topia

# BREWERIANA

We tend to think of beer as an investment in our happiness and well-being rather than a financial one. But there's actually a very robust market for beer-related collectibles, or *breweriana*. There's a network of buyers and sellers around the world dedicated to digging up the rarest, coolest, and most valuable memora-beer-ia they can find.

As with any other collectibles market, pricing fluctuates wildly, and is driven by a slew of occasionally quite subjective criteria, including nostalgia-driven demand. "The older, the better" is a good rule of thumb, and if you happen to have a crate full of pre-Prohibition beer cans sitting in your basement, then you can probably start making retirement plans right now.

If you own **a rare can** made after 1975 or so, odds are it's going to be worth anywhere from 25 cents to a few dollars. The average value of a can

rises with age, with a healthy spike pre-Prohibition, especially if the can is from a smaller regional brewery.

The biggest gets are **"cone top" cans** produced before the advent of the pull tab. Again, regional brewers grab the biggest bucks: Wisconsin's Oshkosh Beer, for example, produced a prototype cone top in 1949 that sold for nearly $28,000. (Younger flat-top cans, while not as pricey, can still go for plenty: In 2003, a can of Clipper Pale from Grace Brothers Brewery went for $19,000.)

For the seriously committed, there's the annual CANvention hosted by the Brewery Collectibles Club of America. Held as a traveling roadshow for breweriana lovers, the CANvention is a colorful, memorabilia-stuffed mecca for anyone who's intoxicated by beery lore. Keep an eye on that checkbook, though: Some in-demand items, like **old brewery lithographs,** can cost in the neighborhood of $75,000.

Beer-Topia

# THE UNITED STATES OF BEER, PART 5

**South Carolina:** Since its 2010 founding, Westbrook Brewing has built a healthy buzz with an audacious approach to flavor that's often exemplified by their anniversary brews, including Mexican Cake Imperial Stout (which is made with vanilla beans, cinnamon sticks, and habañero peppers), as well as newer additions to their evolving lineup, such as their Gose. It debuted in 2012, and helped launch the near-extinct German brew's recent stateside revival.

**South Dakota:** Craft beer represents a relatively small portion of the South Dakota state economy, but that may change in the future thanks to companies like Crow Peak Brewing Company. Their brews are the most widely available SD craft brew—seek out their Pile-O-Dirt Porter, Eleventh Hour IPA, and Bear Butte Brown Ale.

**Tennessee:** An arcane law has kept any brew over 6.25% ABV out of grocery stores or gas stations and has made it hard for local brews to break through. If they do, it'll be due to the efforts of Linus Hall, owner of the Yazoo Brewing Company in Nashville. The largest craft brewer in the state, Yazoo treats drinkers to a variety of memorable offerings, including SUE, a smoked beer the company refers to as a "smoky malt bomb," and Deux Rouges, a barrel-aged sour.

**Texas:** The craft brew industry has evolved enough that for some brewers, it isn't enough to be "craft." Some, like the Jester King Brewery in Austin, focus their efforts on being *artisanal*, or a focus on local ingredients and brewing techniques that rely on native yeast and bacteria. For the consumer, it means distinctive beer, like Jester King's Atrial Rubicite (a fruity barrel-aged sour) and Black Metal Farmhouse Imperial Stout.

**Utah:** A brewery in a state largely populated by teetotalers should have a hard time, but Uinta Brewing Company has beaten the odds. Its beers are available in more than 25 states, and the company's robust line of year-round and seasonal brews (many of them canned) has developed a stellar reputation, particularly Sum'r Ale, Baba Black Lager, and Hop Nosh IPA. Also cool: In 2001, Uinta became the first entirely wind-powered company in Utah.

**Vermont:** Spend a day at Hill Farmstead Brewery in Greensboro. The company produces many acclaimed brews, including their Farmstead Abner Double IPA and Farmstead Ann Saison. But if it's just a pit stop you have in mind, skip right to the Alchemist, located in Waterbury. Its Heady Topper Double IPA is not only one of the better-loved brews in the state, but also boasts some of the more rapturous reviews of any beer *anywhere.*

Beer-Topia

**Virginia:** Situated directly at the nexus of tradition and emerging technologies, Virginia's AleWerks Brewing Company draws on both—their brick-faced brewhouse, located in colonial Williamsburg, comes courtesy of Peter Austin, the godfather of modern microbrewing, and their fermenters are state of the art. That attitude is also reflected in their broad (and growing) line of beer, which offers tradition with a twist, like their Grand Illumination Ale barleywine, Coffeehouse Stout (brewed with Guatemalan coffee), and Bitter Valentine Double IPA.

**Washington:** Start off with a pint from the Fremont Brewing Company in Seattle, where the Kentucky Dark Star offers an excellent imperial oatmeal stout. Elsewhere in town, you can stop by Elysian Brewing, which has brewed up hundreds of beers since opening in 1996, including the acclaimed Hydra hefeweizen, tasty Karma Citra Wet Hop Ale, and delicious seasonal stuff like their Elysian Punkuccino Coffee Pumpkin Ale.

**West Virginia:** It's not just the land of moonshine anymore! In 2009, the state legislature passed a law doubling the allowed alcohol limit in beer. That paved the way for a craft brewing surge that has given rise to companies like Bridge Brew Works in Fayetteville, where the motto is "Brew beer that we want to drink." Start off with a Dun Glen Dubbel and keep on sipping.

**Wisconsin:** By 1900, Wisconsin had a legitimate claim on its nickname of "Beer Capital of the World." That's thanks in part to the wave of German immigrants who populated the state, as well as being the home of big commercial breweries such as Pabst, Miller, Schlitz, and Blatz. Those days are over, but 21st-century craft brewing has given rise to craftier start-ups, including New Glarus Brewing Company. They're known primarily for their fruit beers, but don't let that scare you off—what these brews may lack in high ABV they more than make up for with distinctive flavor. Try their Wild Sour Ale and Wisconsin Belgian Red.

**Wyoming:** The craft brewing explosion came relatively late to Wyoming, but in 2012, production rose more than 30 percent. But while the state can now claim celebrated upstarts like Black Tooth, Freedom's Edge, and Bitter Creek among its success stories, the grandest teton of Wyoming beer remains the Snake River Brewing Company, whose brews claim a long list of impressive awards (including a World Beer Cup Gold Award) and a widening circle of fans eager to belly up for options like the Zonker Stout, Le Serpent Wild Ale, and Pako's IPA.

# WASHINGTON'S TAB

During colonial times, election season was a time for voters to get together and discuss the issues of the day…and get drunk. And although manners of the day proscribed outright campaigning, few saw anything wrong with candidates buying multiple rounds for their would-be constituents.

One noteworthy candidate who made this work to his advantage was young George Washington. After losing one election largely because of his public complaints regarding too many taverns in town, he crushed the polls during the 1758 vote for the Virginia House of Burgesses after he footed the bill for an epic alcoholic free-for-all that included enough booze to provide each voter with roughly a half-gallon of liquor for free. Washington's tab included 46 gallons of beer, and that's only a fraction of what was poured that day. It's kind of a wonder that anyone, including the victorious Washington, remembered to vote.

# THINKING OF BEER

"Milk is for babies. When you grow up, you have to drink beer."

**—Arnold Schwarzenegger**

"You can't be a real country unless you have a beer and an airline. It helps if you have some kind of a football team, or some nuclear weapons, but at the very least you need a beer."

**—Frank Zappa**

"Beauty is in the eye of the beer holder."

**—Kinky Friedman**

"Whiskey's too rough / Champagne costs too much / Vodka puts my mouth in gear / I hope this refrain / Will help me explain / As a matter of fact, I like beer."

**—Tom T. Hall**

"There is no such thing as a bad beer. It's that some taste better than others."

**—Billy Carter**

"Beer, it's the best damn drink in the world."

**—Jack Nicholson**

251

"Beer makes you feel the way you ought to feel without beer."
— **Henry Lawson**

"Whoever drinks beer, he is quick to sleep; whoever sleeps long, does not sin; whoever does not sin, enters heaven! Thus, let us drink beer!"
— **Martin Luther**

"Who cares how time advances? I am drinking ale today."
— **Edgar Allan Poe**

"Without question, the greatest invention in the history of mankind is beer.

Oh, I grant you that the wheel was also a fine invention, but the wheel does not go nearly as well with pizza."
— **Dave Barry**

"God made yeast, as well as dough, and he loves fermentation just as dearly as he loves vegetation."
— **Ralph Waldo Emerson**

"Beer. It always seems like such a good idea, doesn't it? Beer seems like an even better idea after you'd had some beer."
— **Steven Hall**

Beer-Topia

"Sometimes when I reflect on all the beer I drink I feel ashamed. Then I look into the glass and think about the workers in the brewery. If I didn't drink this beer, they might be out of work and their dreams would be shattered. I think, 'It is better to drink this beer and let their dreams come true than be selfish and worry about my liver.'"

**— Jack Handey**

"On victory, you deserve beer, in defeat, you need it."

**— Napoleon**

"Excessive intake of alcohol, as we know, kills brain cells. But naturally, it attacks the slowest and weakest brain cells first. So, regular consumption of beer eliminates the weaker brain cells, making the brain a faster and more efficient machine. That's why you always feel smarter after a few beers."

**— Cliff Clavin**

"There is more to life than beer alone, but beer makes those other things even better."

**— Stephen Morris**

"I would kill everyone in this room for a drop of sweet beer."
— **Homer Simpson**

"Give a man a beer, waste an hour. Teach a man to brew, and waste a lifetime!"
— **Bill Owen**

"Whiskey and beer are a man's worst enemies, but the man that runs away from his enemies is a coward!"
— **Zeca Pagodinho**

"I'm gaining weight the right way: I'm drinking beer."
— **Johnny Damon**

"Let a man walk 10 miles steadily on a hot summer's day along a dusty English road, and he will soon discover why beer was invented."
— **G.K. Chesterton**

"Not all chemicals are bad. Without chemicals such as hydrogen and oxygen, there would be no way to make a water, a vital ingredient in beer."
— **Dave Barry**

"Those who drink beer will think beer."
— **Washington Irving**

Beer-Topia

# ANSWERS

**For "Hooray Beer!" from page 192**

**1.** m; **2.** l; **3.** i; **4.** a; **5.** g; **6.** t; **7.** h; **8.** s; **9.** r; **10.** p; **11.** c; **12.** q; **13.** d; **14.** k; **15.** f; **16.** e; **17.** n; **18.** o; **19.** u; **20.** j; **21.** b

**For "Can't Get Enough of That Wonderful Duff" from page 238**

**1.** o; **2.** n; **3.** l; **4.** k: **5.** j; **6.** p; **7.** c; **8.** m; **9.** b; **10.** h; **11.** i; **12.** q; **13.** e; **14.** g; **15.** d; **16.** a; **17.** f

# BATHROOM READERS—
# THEY JUST DON'T GET ANY
# BETTER THAN THIS.

Contact us at:
**Bathroom Readers' Institute**
P.O. Box 1117
Ashland, OR 97520

# THE LAST PAGE

### Fellow Bathroom Readers:

The fight for good bathroom reading should never be taken loosely—we must do our duty and sit firmly for what we believe in, even while the rest of the world is taking potshots at us.

We'll be brief. Now that we've proven we're not simply a flush-in-the-pan, we invite you to take the plunge:

Sit Down and Be Counted! Log on to www.bathroomreader.com and earn a permanent spot on the BRI honor roll!

If you like reading our books...VISIT THE BRI'S WEBSITE!
www.bathroomreader.com

- Receive our irregular newsletters via e-mail
- Order additional Bathroom Readers
- Face us on Facebook
- Tweet us on Twitter
- Blog us on our blog

Go with the Flow...

Well, we're out of space, and when you've gotta go, you've gotta go. Tanks for all your support. Hope to hear from you soon.

Meanwhile, remember...

### KEEP ON FLUSHIN'!

Beer-Topia